I0830830

THE ULTIMATE ALPHA MALE

HOW TO TURN YOUR INTIMACY ISSUES INTO BALL BUSTING SUPERPOWERS AND BECOME A TOTAL SEXUAL WARRIOR

By

Bryan Bruce

MY GIFT TO YOU CLICK THE LINK BELOW

https://nowthis.life/rac/

PLEASE WRITE A REVIEW!

If this book helped you out in anyway, please help me to help others by writing a review!

https://www.amazon.com/dp/B073S7Y435

Still, if you did not get anything new from this book or you were not impacted in some way, I would still like to hear what you have to say. Either way, I will know what am doing right or wrong and to improve in the future. I wouldn't like to take your money and not deliver. So please, take just 2 minutes to let me know what you think.

Everyone is searching for help on how to improve their lives for the better and one thing they do look for are reviews. If this book has a lot amazing reviews with great comments, they will buy the book and read it and so the ripples effects of goodness spreads. But if it doesn't have any great reviews and comments, they don't buy the book and read it.

I know this book can positively impact and help someone and you can help that person by writing your thoughts and takeaways from the book.

Additionally, I would like to read your review and hear how this book has helped you in anyway at shape or form. My plan is to print every single review and hang them on my home office wall to read for inspiration and motivation throughout the day.

Your great review helps me personally to stay focused and be able to validate all the hard work and lots of hours invested in preparing this book for you.

https://www.amazon.com/dp/B073S7Y435

Thank you again for reading this book and all of your support, I am truly honored and grateful to have been of help. I look forward to helping you make this year the best ever for you and your family!

OTHER BOOKS BY BRYAN

The Female Logic

When You Suck At Dating

Legal Disclaimer
Although the information in this book may be very helpful, it is sold with the understanding that neither the author nor the publisher is engaged in presenting specific psychological, emotional, or sexual advice. Nor is anything in this book intended to be a diagnosis, prescription, recommendation, or cure for any specific kind of psychological, emotional, or sexual problem. Each individual has unique needs and this book cannot take into account each of these differences.

TABLE OF CONTENTS

INTRODUCTION

In this book, you will discover the fastest, easiest and most powerful ways to attract beautiful women on the deepest level possible.

You may not believe that you can do it until you use the techniques from this program and see it happening before your own eyes. Get ready to experience success with the types of women you've always wanted.

You will discover how to behave, how to talk, what body language to use and what vibe to have so you easily get along with that crowd. You'll also learn how to make them want to be your friend and want you to stick around and be a part of the group.

I will talk about the four most important types of presence: Assertive presence, sexual presence, relaxed presence and loving presence.

Get ready to experience a completely new level of success with women! You will be simply amazed at what happens when you use these techniques around women.

If you take a close look at many of the most successful people in the world over the course of history, you will see that the majority of these iconic men and women were firm believers in the power of their inner spirit or intuition (God within).

In other words, they knew to trust their gut. They lived by the "no matter what" mentality, surrounded themselves with like-minded folks, believed in positive affirmation and prayer, and took inspired daily action on getting what they wanted in life.

They didn't complain, whine, or blame anyone for anything they didn't achieve. They took full responsibility for themselves, trusted their gut, and took inspired action towards creating the lives they wanted.

In this book, you will discover the secrets to deepening your confidence to levels that you simply cannot imagine right now. This will not only help you with women, but in all areas of life.

Please note that inspired daily action is very different from taking forceful action in an attempt to make things happen or speed up the process of manifestation of whatever it is you want.

Forceful action creates a lower energetic vibration and does not allow for an energetic match with what you want or your "desire."

Attempting to force what you want into form rather than standing strong in your faith and honoring the messages you receive from your intuition will cause a low energetic vibration that will only delay its manifestation.

Inspired action will create a vibrational match for what you want and your inner spirit, and that match will move you to manifestation.

Start by taking time to recognize, understand, and connect with your intuition. Spend quiet, uninterrupted time with yourself, clear your head of mind chatter, take some nice deep breaths, and be creative in asking for guidance on whatever you'd like help with.

For instance, if you would like general guidance, simply ask "What do I need to know today?" If you want help with something more specific, ask "What's my next step to...?" and complete the question with whatever the specific thing is you need help with.

With practice, you'll discover the endless stream of ideas and guidance your intuition may offer in these precious quiet times.

Be patient with yourself and the process. In the early stages you'll likely find your logical mind chattering away, making it difficult to relax and focus.

Just let the mind chatter pass and focus again on listening and observing. You may receive a response quickly or it may come to you later in the day when you least expect it.

As you improve your ability and understanding, you will recognize these intuitive responses.

So put these elements in motion and set your sights high- the higher the better! Trust your gut and remember the extreme importance of expressing your sincere gratitude for all of your blessings.

With this combination and your strong faith, you, too, may join the ranks of the "no matter what" mentality and manifest everything you want.

CHAPTER ONE

TRUSTING YOUR LIFE: HOW TO MAKE YOUR LIFE COMPLETELY TRUSTWORTHY AND INDESTRUCTIBLE

What is an alpha male? If the term confuses you, then allow me to give you the simple understanding of what an alpha male truly is. The alpha male is the leader of the pack; the man amongst men as most people would say it.

Just like a pack of wild wolves in a hunt, the alpha male is the one that leads. If you are in a party or in a social event and if you notice a particular guy who walks in confidently amongst his peers while the women look at him in awe and admiration.

That is your alpha male. Always oozing with confidence, these guys are a rare breed indeed.

Why are they called the alpha male? Think about it! These guys can charm their way into the hearts of any woman that they want! I bet you would like to become one, right? Well, that would depend on how you live your life right now.

Are you someone who can talk to and make any woman comfortable yet nervous around you? Are you a guy who can instantly pick up women from inside a bar or a party with the use of a few words and some actions?

If your answers to these questions are "YES", then you are a naturally born alpha male! But the painful truth out there is that there is NO SUCH THING as a naturally born alpha!

Alpha men are made, not born; there are certain alpha male characteristics that you need to possess or grow within you before you can become the real deal.

I'm sitting here thinking about life and the infinite abundance that is available to us and I see many opportunities to feel happy, create wealth, and experience love and connections with others.

The biggest thing that keeps people restricted from accessing this high level of abundance is that they 'rarely' trust in life.

When you mistrust someone, you also cut yourself off from the great emotions you can share.

But as you begin to trust people, you find greater positive experiences begin to unfold.

Now this is also the same in your life abundance too.
Consider for a second, do you trust in your dreams to come true?
Do you trust your positive experiences? Do you trust new opportunities life has to offer? Do you trust yourself to bring about the manifestation of your dreams? Do you trust God?

The more you trust in life's beautiful manifestation, the more you'll feel connected to it's creation.

Trust will tie you into abundance because your faith and belief will align with it.

So begin TO TRUST EVERYTHING THAT'S GOOD IN YOUR LIFE!

Trust in yourself... your body, your health, your positive emotions, your positive thoughts and your positive experiences... past, present and future.

You'll find that the more you trust in life, the more your mind will begin to establish a personal connection with what you want to manifest.

Make sure you build on your faith and convince yourself that your life is the truest manifestation of the abundance you feel around you - and realize all good is connected to you as a human being.

Trust the abundance you see everyday and connect with it.

Would you like to improve your life in one or more areas? Are you aware of and living your life purpose? Do you have difficulty making decisions?

Well, learning to use your intuition can definitely help you with all of these things and more! Intuition has been referred to by many different names including your inner voice, a gut feeling, your higher self, a "knowing", instinct or having a hunch.

It is something that everyone knows of and probably has had some type of experience with, but few people actually understand or consciously use. It is like having your own personal compass to direct you which way to go, especially when you come to a crossroads or become lost in life.

You may have a big decision to make or be searching for answers or be unhappy about something in your life and want your life to be more meaningful and fulfilling. Learning to use your intuition can make your life easier by helping you make better decisions that are more in tune with who you are. It is as easy as following a few simple steps.

Steps To Following Your Intuition
There are basically 3 simple steps to following your intuition.
1- Listen to intuitive messages.
2- Trust the messages that you receive.
3- Follow or act upon the messages or guidance that you receive.

Step 1 - Listen

The first step to following your intuition is to learn how to listen to it. You have probably had many intuitive feelings or hunches during your life that you may or may not be aware of.

You may not have "heard' or paid attention to them though, thinking that they were just some other random thought. Most of the time intuition tends to be subtle, like someone whispering in your ear or a brief feeling you have about something, for no apparent reason.

It also tends to happen and you are more likely to hear it, when you are quiet or alone, as this is when your conscious mind becomes more quiet or your thinking slows down.

When you are not busy doing many different tasks or being distracted and preoccupied with things outside of yourself, you have an opportunity to relax and turn down the number of your thoughts.

Some Specific Ways To Listen To or "Hear" Your Intuition Better

Spend some time by yourself or doing relaxing activities. Be fully present in the moment, while doing habitual activities or regular tasks. Listen to music and dance freely.

Do individual physical activities like yoga or walking. Spend time outside in nature - go for a walk, sit beneath a tree. Spend time in, near or around water - take a bath, sit by a stream, go swimming. Meditate regularly. Pay attention to "signs" or answers in your daily life.

2 - Trust

Trust is very important in every relationship in your life. The most important relationship you have, is with yourself. Trusting yourself and your intuition gives you strong self confidence, as you believe in yourself and the decisions you make.

So, learning to trust your intuition is the next the lesson in using your intuition. Once you have heard your intuition or experienced a "gut feeling", you need to be able to trust it and believe it, even if it does not make sense at the time.

Your "rational" or conscious mind may tend to get in the way with all your inner dialogue and random thoughts. You may question, doubt or ignore the intuitive ideas or information that you receive, often thinking it is just another random thought.

Paying attention to how you feel about the intuitive information is the key to trusting it. Trusting your intuition can be the most challenging step as your old beliefs and doubts can be strong.

It can be hard to believe the information that you receive is true. Tune into how you feel about the idea, information or guidance. If it feels right or wrong, have faith, trust and go with that feeling.

3 - Follow

So, this is where you actually take action and follow your intuitive guidance. You may still question or doubt your intuition but you want to ignore those thoughts and take action anyway! Act on the information that you receive and then pay attention to how you feel afterward to see if it was your intuition or if you confused it with fear or doubt. The more you practice, the more in tune you will become with identifying what your intuition or gut feeling feels like to you.

Everyone is a little different in how they experience their intuition. Learning to listen to, trust and follow your intuition is just like learning any new skill, so you need to practice it in order to become better.

One approach that may help is to take action and follow your intuition right away, before your conscious mind has had a chance to confuse you with a million other thoughts, doubts or questions. Then assess how you felt.

These are the 3 simple steps to following your intuition and the more you practice using them the better your results will be. Thanks a lot for your interest and taking the time to read this guide. I sincerely hope you really enjoyed it! Remember that knowledge is useless, until you apply it, so I strongly encourage you to do so!

Trust Your Instincts

The daily punishment you can place your body & mind under - as a result of constant negative feedback - can leave you with a lack of trust in your inner instincts. You can learn over time that it's not safe to trust that inner voice that tells you it's time to speak up (particularly when there is a chance you may get hurt).

Why might you feel insecure in your ability to trust your instincts?

Often this happens as a result of rejections and others letting you down. When you are rejected by someone you love you can easily learn (incorrectly) that you are not a worthy person and also learn that your instincts about this person were not accurate. You can begin to wonder if you really can trust your guidance system that has led you into a situation where pain has been the outcome.

Add to this when those you care about regularly let you down, you can learn not to trust your inner guidance system who once again led you to these relationships.

What we tend to quickly forget is that 99.9% of times your inner voice has tried to warn you about others who may not be the best 'fit' for you, but you have allowed your desires 'in the moment' to drive your behaviour and hence pushed forward with people who time and time again let you down.

The question you need to ask yourself is "when will I start to realise the importance of listening to my instincts?"

When you repeatedly ignore your inner voice you leave yourself vulnerable. You are vulnerable to:

1- Being hurt by those who do not truly show you the respect you deserve

2- Ignoring potential errors that could lead to future problems

3- Rejecting opportunities to stretch your wings and be the person you truly want to be

4- Not standing up for yourself

5- Others developing an inaccurate picture of you

So you can see, learning to pay attention when your intuition is trying to speak up, is vital to your overall health, happiness and success in life.

Start today!

Start to listen to your inner voice. Don't rush into decisions. Give yourself time and permission to do things in your own time. Don't ignore your inner drives - particularly out of fear. Act - when your instincts tell you to speak up.

Trust your instincts - one instinct at a time!

CHAPTER TWO

CLEARING YOUR SHAME AND USING IT TO YOUR ADVANTAGE: PART 1

When you're embarrassment you feel somewhat uneasy, maybe ashamed, somewhat humiliated and kind of self-conscious. On the surface we don't normally classify embarrassment as a fear, however for the purpose of this discussion it's important to look at it in this way.

Embarrassment often manifests when a weakness or an inadequacy has been made public. You might also feel ashamed because you're feeling guilty about something you did that has now become public knowledge.

Likewise you might end up feeling ashamed when you're caught doing something that is socially unacceptable. These events can often make you feel incredibly uncomfortable and self-conscious. All of a sudden the hidden secrets you've been holding close to your heart are now in the public realm.

It's just difficult to bear. You are now open to judgment, ridicule, rejection and criticism. All of a sudden it seems as though embarrassment isn't the only fear you have to deal with.

You've probably heard the saying that some people have absolutely no shame. These are the kinds of people that don't often concern themselves with what others think or say about them.

These are the kinds of people who never get ashamed and

are often very open about every aspect of their lives. They don't care about being rejected or criticized. In fact, they seem to revel in the fact that other people don't approve of their decisions, actions or behavior.

They think this way because they feel comfortable and secure in their own skin. They are confident and have high levels of self-esteem and self-belief.

In contrast, a person who is afraid of being ashamed is often very insecure. They have very low levels of self-esteem, and they are always fearing judgment, ridicule and criticism. These are the kinds of people who often try to please others.

They try their hardest to live up to other people's expectations of them. However, they tend to feel that they are not quite good enough. As a result they are afraid to make mistakes and afraid of failing.

This makes them hesitant in their actions and that is when the fear of embarrassment manifests in their lives.

Suffering from the fear of embarrassment can actually be quite debilitating. It will tend to stifle your confidence while completely undermining your social and personal growth.

It will discourage you from taking the necessary risks that will help you take advantage of opportunities and get ahead in this world, and it will prevent you from attempting new things.

You will rarely if ever step outside your comfort zone because you fear that you will not look favorable in other people's eyes. It could also very well be that you're somewhat of a perfectionist.

Unless you do things perfectly, you will never be good enough. And if you're not good enough, then obviously that makes you a failure.

The Perfectionist Trap

It's important to understand that nobody is perfect. Perfection is only an opinion. What's perfect for one person is far from perfect for another person.

Therefore perfection depends entirely on the standards you set yourself and on the expectations you have of yourself in the situation you are attempting to work through.

The moment you lower your standards and expectations and make them more realistic and achievable is the moment you will begin ridding yourself of the fear of embarrassment.

In fact, it's important to remind yourself that everyone makes mistakes. Mistakes are a part of life. For this very reason it's critical to allow yourself room to make mistakes and to fail at times. Everything that happens is simply a learning experience, and other people will often respect that.

We all know that nobody else is perfect. We all know that everyone makes mistakes. We all know that people fail at times. In fact, often when trying new things, people fail more often then they succeed.

However, it's the growth that we get from our failures and mistakes that makes all the difference in the end. It's this growth that helps us gain the experience and confidence we need to do things better the next time around.

Subdue Your Critical Voice

When it comes to making mistakes, failing and feeling ashamed, it's important to understand that you are always your biggest critic. You might think that other people will judge and criticize you. Yes, some people might, but most people won't.

Most people will actually empathize with you. They will relate with what you're going through because at one time or another they were in exactly your position. Yes, events and circumstances might have been different.

However, they were certainly there making mistakes and feeling somewhat embarrassed and ashamed of themselves. It's all normal. In fact, you might be surprised that many of these people might not even care less.

They are so absorbed in their own world and in their own problems that they might only give you a few moments of their conscious attention.

Given all this, the reality is that it's not other people who make you feel self-conscious, it's rather your own critical voice that is creating these problems.

Consider for a moment that what makes you feel ashamed actually inspires and excites another person. Or, how about what makes you feel embarrassed actually challenges and motivates someone else.

Therefore embarrassment isn't so much what happens to you, but rather how you interpret what happens to you. And all this comes back to that critical voice inside your head that is making you feel absolutely miserable.

Prepare yourself to tune-out that critical voice, and move forward with greater confidence.

What to do Before Embarrassment Strikes

There are certain things you can do before you step into an uncomfortable situation where you might feel a little ashamed and uncertain.

The guidelines that follow will hopefully provide you with a variety of ways you can potentially prepare yourself for moments of embarrassment — helping you handle those awkward moments far more effectively.

At this stage, it's all about building your anti-embarrassment muscle. This muscle must be flexed and strengthened, so that when you go out into the world you can bear the brunt of the challenges that life throws your way.

Subdue Your Expectations

The first thing you must do is subdue your expectations. If your expectations provide you with no room to make mistakes and goof up a little, then you're simply setting yourself up for failure.

It's therefore important to subdue the expectations you have about yourself and the expectations you have about yourself in this particular situation. Ask yourself:

1- What are my expectations?
2- What expectations do I have of myself?
3- What expectations do I have of myself in this particular situation?
4- Are my expectations realistic and reasonable?
5- Do they allow me room to make mistakes?
6- How could I reasonably adjust my expectations?

Be open to the fact that you will make mistakes. Mistakes are a normal and natural part of life. It's okay to goof up. In fact you shouldn't be ashamed when things don't turn out as expected.

Everyone is fallible, and nobody is ever perfect no matter how things may appear to be on the surface. You must therefore accept the fact that mistakes will be made and as such you must let go of your perfectionist nature.

7- It's okay that I'm not perfect...
8- It's okay to make mistakes...
9- It's perfectly okay to fail as long as I learn from this experience...

Feel comfortable in the fact that you are imperfect. Every mistake you make you will learn from and do better next time.

Learn to Handle Fear

Embarrassment is a type of fear. It's closely tied to the fear of uncertainty, rejection and criticism. Once you learn to handle these fears successfully, you will feel far more confident when stepping into uncomfortable situations that might potentially embarrass you.

Spend time learning how to handle the following types of fear:

Fear or rejection
Fear of criticism
Fear of failure
Fear of success
Fear of making mistakes
Fear of uncertainty

And any other fear you feel is getting in your way.

As you build your fear muscle you will suddenly gain more certainty, and with certainty will come motivation and confidence. And that could be all you need to handle your feelings of embarrassment.

Preparation and Attention to Detail

It's paramount that you focus on developing two critical things. First, you must develop your mental alertness and awareness. This is important because while performing certain tasks and activities you will need to be mentally alert and aware of everything that is going on around you.

When you're in this mental state of awareness you will be far more likely to change direction at a moments notice and respond to unexpected events and circumstances.

What this really means is that you are less likely to get ashamed because you are paying attention to all the details. There will be no surprises because you are ready for everything and flexible enough to change your decisions, behavior and actions at a moments notice.

Developing alertness and awareness comes with time.

However, the most important thing you can do is to learn to be more mindful.

Be mindful of the moment, and pay attention to the process of how you're doing things. Also be mindful of the results you get from doing these things and how this effects and influences the things around you.

The second thing you must do that will reduce the likelihood of feeling ashamed is to prepare yourself thoroughly. The more thoroughly you are prepared, the more confident and capable you will be and the less likely you are to make a mistake and get ashamed.

Just spend time preparing yourself. However be careful not to over-prepare and get lost in the details. Don't fall into the perfectionist trap. Prepare enough so that you come to understand what is required of you to ready yourself for the challenges you might face along the way.

Examine Your Limiting Beliefs

You might very well be prone to feeling ashamed because you have a number of limiting beliefs about specific situations, or about your ability to handle your emotions within a specific situation.

One way to overcome your limiting beliefs is to begin questioning the validity of each belief. Actually spend time throwing doubts upon these beliefs by asking yourself:

1- What belief is causing me to feel ashamed?
2- What do I believe about myself or about the situation I find myself in?
3- Is this a realistic belief to have?
4- What doesn't make sense about this belief?
5- Where's the evidence that disproves this belief?
6- Who could provide me with another perspective that could disprove this belief?

Gain other people's perspectives and thoughts about your beliefs. Listen to what they say. You might be surprised with how they view things. Maybe your belief is not as legitimate as you originally made it out to be.

Work on Developing Your Confidence

The more confidence you have in yourself and your own ability, the less likely you are to feel ashamed. It's actually a fact that the more confidence someone has, the less likely they are to succumb to the fear or criticism, rejection, making mistakes and failure.

It takes a lot to make a confident person feel ashamed because they feel comfortable in their own skin and they are willing to take the necessary risks to step outside their comfort zone, to expand their horizons and stretch themselves in a variety of ways.

It's also a fact that the more knowledge and experience you gain, the more confident you will feel about yourself and your circumstances. Confidence essentially comes through trial and error.

It comes from making mistakes and learning from them. You might not know what to do initially, however over time you learn and grow from your experience, and this provides you with the confidence you need to move forward successfully.

Purposefully Put Yourself in Uncomfortable Situations

To strengthen your levels of confidence and to build that anti-embarrassment muscle you must purposefully put yourself into uncomfortable situations.

An uncomfortable situation means something that is likely to make you feel somewhat uneasy and potentially embarrassed. Of course initially it's important not to do this with things that have significant meaning in your life.

Instead do it with less important things. For instance, how about playing a new sport you haven't played before. Initially you probably won't be very good, but who really cares.

You'll make mistakes, embarrass yourself, laugh it off and have some fun. Nobody cares, and you shouldn't care either. Use this experience to build your anti-embarrassment muscle. And then the next week do something else uncomfortable.

Hopefully over time you will realize that embarrassment is just a little bit of fun. It's a learning experience. Everyone gets ashamed and it's not really a big deal.

Visualize Yourself Handling Embarrassment

The subconscious mind can't tell the difference between something that is real and something that is only imagined in your mind. This is very important because it means that you can work through embarrassing moments first in your imagination before tackling them in the real world.

In fact the more you visualize yourself successfully and calmly handling an embarrassing moment in your imagination, the more confidence you will have in yourself to be able to tackle this situation much more effectively in the real world.

Take some time to sit in a quiet place and close your eyes. Visualize all the events and circumstances surrounding this activity you are embarrassed about and see everything working out in your favor.

However, all of a sudden something unexpected happens and you feel a little ashamed. Your emotions could easily and quickly get out of control. However, you calmly center yourself, subdue your emotions and laugh things off. You bring a light-hearted nature into everything you do, and as a result it's very difficult for you to feel ashamed.

Prepare for Future Embarrassment

Moving on from the previous point, take time to reflect on all the ways you've been ashamed in the past. Have a good think about the specific situations that have made you feel uneasy.

Within these situations are lessons you must learn that may very well help you in the present moment. Also have a think about all the things you might potentially feel ashamed about in the future. Ask yourself:

- What could potentially embarrass me in the future?
- How will I respond during these moments?
- How must I prepare myself to successfully and calmly handle these circumstances?

By visualizing all the different possible embarrassing scenarios that you could potentially confront in the future, and then picturing in your mind how you will work through them successfully will help you to gain the confidence you need to make better decisions moving forward.

Then when it comes time to do the real thing in the real world, you will be ready for anything that might come your way. Preparation is the key.

CHAPTER THREE

CLEARING YOUR SHAME AND USING IT TO YOUR ADVANTAGE: PART 2

What to do During Moments of Embarrassment

Okay, so you've done all this prior work to help build that anti-embarrassment muscle. In fact, you feel as though you've prepared as thoroughly as you possibly could.

You've learned how to handle different types of fears, you've subdued your expectations, worked on developing your confidence, spent time visualizing handling embarrassing moments calmly and successfully, and even purposefully put yourself into uncomfortable and potentially embarrassing situations in an attempt to desensitize yourself emotionally.

However, now you're faced with the real thing. Something has happened, you feel somewhat uncertain and you are on the verge of one of the most embarrassing moments of your life. What to do?

Here are some guidelines and suggestions to help you handle the fear of embarrassment in the moment.

Stay Calm, Cool and Collected

The most important things you must do is stay cool, calm and collected. Take several deep breaths, count backwards from ten and settle yourself down by coming back to the present moment.

Within these critical few moments become mindful of where you are, what you're doing, and of your immediate surroundings.

Don't regret the past or worry about the future.

Just settle in the present moment. When you become aware of the moment you will no longer be thinking about other people or about what you're feeling ashamed about. Instead you will be focused on yourself and on the peaceful sound of your breath.

Take Responsibility

The second most important thing you must do during these uncomfortable moments is to take responsibility for what just happened. Don't deny what happened, don't try to hide behind your flaws or mistakes. Just take responsibility for what you did and for what transpired.

It doesn't even matter if it's not your fault. You're in this situation, and you must now gracefully work through this situation successfully. Blaming, chucking a tantrum or shamelessly walking away will not help you here.

If you made a mistake, own up to it. If something unexpected happened that made you feel uncomfortable, then embrace these circumstances. You can't change what happened. However, you can most certainly begin anew right now in this very moment.

Think Positively and Creatively

The third most important thing is to think positively and creatively about the situation.

Yes, of course you might be in a little bit of a pickle. Things are uncomfortable and you are feeling somewhat ashamed. It's important not to allow your emotions to get the better of you.

As such, it's critical that you think positively. Maybe things aren't as bad as you initially made them out to be. Maybe you could put a positive spin on this situation. And just maybe this is a perfect opportunity in disguise.

Staying optimistic and viewing the situation in a positive light will immediately open a world of possibilities. No longer will you be the victim of circumstance, but instead you will become the master of your own destiny.

Once you're in control, begin thinking creatively about how you will get through this situation successfully. You can for instance do this by envisioning yourself as a comedian on stage entertaining people. A comedian makes mistakes, goofs up and as a result stimulates laughter.

Maybe you just need to laugh at yourself to help ease the tension you are feeling. If that's not appropriate in your situation, then alternatively imagine yourself as an actor acting out a role in a movie. See yourself acting out a script within a movie.

This might very well help desensitize you from the events and circumstances. And finally, how about imagining yourself as a cartoon character? What would Bart Simpson do in your situation? Actually maybe that's not such a great example.

Don't Take Yourself too Seriously

Moving on from the previous point, it's important not to take yourself too seriously. You will goof up, things will happen unexpectedly and that's all okay.

It's not so much what happens to you but rather how you respond to what happens that makes all the difference in the end.

And how you respond to an embarrassing situation should be relaxed and light-hearted. Learn to laugh at your mistakes, circumstances and mishaps. Don't get upset over trivial matters.

Consider for a moment that what seems embarrassing for you, might not at all be embarrassing for others. For all you know, other people haven't even noticed your mistakes or mishaps.

Or maybe they have absolutely no idea why you would be feeling ashamed about these circumstances in the first place. These are all legitimate perspectives. However, you will never get to the point of seeing things this way if you take yourself too seriously.

Don't Succumb to Peer Expectations

Everyone has their own personal standards and expectations of themselves and of others. You can't change this. Other people are entitled to have their own opinions and viewpoints.

They are free to expect certain things from you, however this doesn't mean that you must put external pressure on yourself to meet other people's expectations of you.

Instead clarify your own expectations, live up to your own standards, and do things at your own pace and in your own way.

Don't Retaliate Defensively

If you're criticized, laughed at or judged, it's important you don't retaliate negatively or defensively. Don't blame other people for what happened. Don't lash out angrily.

Emotional outbursts can only make the situation much more unbearable and can potentially make you feel regretful and even more ashamed. Instead control your emotional responses, be open to the possibilities and take responsibility for keeping a cool head.

Don't Focus on Embarrassing Circumstances

Once the embarrassing moment has passed, just move on with what you need to do. There is no point in dwelling on things. You probably have better things to do, and you have the rest of your life to live.

Don't allow this one moment to ruin the rest of your day, your week or even the remainder of this year. It's not worth it.

Accept that it happened, learn from the experience, but don't obsess yourself with endless regrets and "what if" scenarios. This is never helpful and will just effect other areas of your life in negative ways.

What to do After You Have Been Embarrassed

Finally, the moment of embarrassment has passed. You're out in the clear and can move on with your life. Well, at least that should be the case. However, many people continue to re-live their embarrassing moments in their imaginations for days, weeks, months and sometimes years.

In fact, some people never seem to get over the shame and/or embarrassment they felt in that moment. Their entire lives are now in an emotional ruin and all of a sudden they have these phobias where they can no longer bear to see themselves in certain situations.

This is not good. It's not good because these phobias don't only affect them in specific situations, they now tend to expand into other areas of their lives ruining their relationships, career prospects and health. It's certainly no way to live.

Living with the fear of embarrassment is never helpful. It can actually be very debilitating and hurtful in the long-run. What happened, happened. You either dealt with the situation successfully and calmly, or you didn't. Nothing can be changed. At least nothing in the past. However, you can certainly learn from your experience and use it to help lay a stronger foundation for the future.

So whether you completely ashamed yourself, or managed to work through an embarrassing situation successfully and calmly, you will hopefully find the following guidelines helpful to help you gain the most from every potentially embarrassing experience.

Forgive Yourself

No matter what happened, no matter how you responded, and no matter what ended up transpiring, it's very important you forgive yourself and walk away with no regrets.

It is only through forgiveness that you will be able to move on with your life. Holding onto things will only hold you back and prevent you from moving forward. Living with regret doesn't help anyone feel better in the long-term.

Stop Apologizing for Your Mistakes

It's important to keep reminding yourself that you're not perfect, and never will be perfect. Perfection is all in the eye of the beholder. What looks like perfection for one person is far from perfect for another person.

Therefore stop apologizing for your mistakes. Instead, embrace your mistakes. Mistakes are powerful learning tools you can use to help you make better choices and decisions in the future.

Distract Yourself Mentally

Initially it might be difficult to get the embarrassing event and circumstances out of your head. In fact, you might at the moment be blowing them out of proportion in your imagination.

That's perfectly okay and understandable. In such instances give yourself permission to distract yourself temporarily from such thoughts so that you can get on with the rest of your life — up until the moment you can take the time to reflect on what happened and learn from the experience.

The most important thing is not to allow these embarrassing circumstances to eat away at other areas of your life including your relationships with others, your career, your health, and personal achievement.

There are numerous harmless ways you can distract yourself. For instance you can distract yourself through exercise, by socializing, or listening to your favorite uplifting music, etc.

However, it's important to keep in mind that these are only temporary distractions that give you time to settle yourself down.

Once you've settled down, it's critical you take time to have a think about what happened and analyze the situation to help improve your circumstances the next time around.

As a side note, it's important not to indulge in addictions as a form of distraction. These forms of distraction will often interfere with important areas of your life and can actually make your circumstances far more complicated.

Take Time to Contemplate

In order to grow from the experience you must learn from the experience. And in order to learn from the experience you must be open to the possibilities and you must be willing to change.

Take time to have a good think about the events that took place that led to the moment of embarrassment. Ask yourself:

1- What happened?
2- How did I respond to what happened?
3- Was I careless or simply unprepared? Why?
4- What was funny about the situation?
5- What can I learn from this experience?
6- What will I do differently the next time around?

It's important to note down and analyze whether you were simply careless or unprepared. A lack of preparation and carelessness might very well have been the cause of your embarrassment.

If unprepared, then you might need to prepare more thoroughly the next time around so that you have a clearer understanding of what you need to do. If on the other hand you were careless, then you might need to be more aware, focused and mindful of the moment.

Either way you are encouraging yourself to think more thoughtfully about your circumstances, and this can only help build your confidence moving forward.

Gain a Different Perspective of the Situation

So far you've probably only viewed your embarrassing situation one way and this might be making you feel absolutely miserable. However, consider the possibility that there are a number of different ways you could potentially view this embarrassing moment. Ask yourself:

1- How else could I view this situation?
2- How could seeing things this way be of value?

Maybe seeing things as an experiment or as a performance of some sort may help you shift your perspective about the situation in a more positive and helpful way. It doesn't even matter if these viewpoints make any sense.

Just maybe seeing things in a slightly different light will open up the possibility that things are not as bad as they initially seemed to be. And this can provide you with the hope you need to approach the situation more confidently the next time around.

Gain Inspiration from Others

If you're stuck on ideas and unable to find new and helpful perspectives to help you reconstruct your embarrassing moment, then it's always helpful to have a chat with other people to gain their perspectives and opinions.

In fact, find a trusted friend and share your embarrassing moment with them. Let them have a little bit of a chuckle, and don't hesitate to share their laughter. This might very well help you relax and settle down your runaway thoughts.

Once the initial laughter dies down, ask your friend to share their own embarrassing stories. Maybe there are some valuable lessons within their experience that you could potentially use to feel better about your own experience.

In the end we always learn best through stories. When you share stories of your own life experiences with others, you learn from the act of sharing and listening to other people's perspectives and opinions.

And when others share stories with you, you also learn as you try and put yourself in their shoes and live through their experience in your own way. Then you take the lessons and try to apply them into your own life.

That's how we learn. And that's how you must learn to overcome your fear of embarrassment.

CHAPTER FOUR

GETTING RIGHT WITH YOUR COCK

Men are particularly bad at piping up about health issues, especially when it comes to our penises. Often, a source of embarrassment can be a simple lack of knowledge. Fortunately, the male anatomy is quite easy to understand, and learning what to say when seeing your GP can help avoid red faces.

Don't use slang
The number of highly imaginative slang words that have been used to describe cocks can leave patients embarrassed and doctors wondering. Keep it real and you'll be taken seriously. Here's a quick anatomically correct dictionary of my own for you to memorise and check off next time you're in the mirror:

Glans/tip - the highly sensitive area at the end of the cock, usually covered by a foreskin, unless removed in an operation called a circumcision, with an opening for urine and semen to escape.

Meatus - pronounced "me-ay-tuss", this is the medical name for that opening.

Glans/tip - the highly sensitive area at the end of the penis, usually covered by a foreskin, unless removed in an operation called a circumcision, with an opening for urine and semen to escape.

Meatus - pronounced "me-ay-tuss", this is the medical name for that opening.

Testes - otherwise known as testicles or balls. All are acceptable.

Scrotum - this is the stretchy skin that forms a sack for your testes. A thin muscle allows the scrotum to contract, which it does so in cold conditions to maintain your sperm at a constant temperature.

Epididymis - behind and above the testes lies the area that stores the sperm made in the testes. Above the testes is a firm tube that carries your sperm from the epididymis (via the prostate which lies near your bladder, so it goes a long way) eventually out through your urethra to come out in the hole in the tip of your cock yep, the meatus - well remembered).

Knowing just a small detail of anatomy can really take the embarrassment out of a problem when explaining things. So next time you notice that something's not right, be confident and just tell your doctor "straight up".

How to clean your penis
We often gaze in awe and talk excitedly about the nose-tingling, fungus-coated, ash-rolled, squishy goodness that is a well-stocked cheese counter. That's not what you want people to experience when getting up close and personal with your penis.

The "knob cheese" that is technically known as smegma, has a particularly vile smell and builds up when the area underneath a foreskin hasn't been cleaned.

This area should be cleaned daily (just pull back) along with the rest of your genitals, your bottom and the area in between, called the perineum. Use a mild soap as these areas can be sensitive.

How to examine your scrotum
Testicular cancer is the most common cancer in young men. For this reason, every week you should examine each testis (the

plural is testes) in turn between your finger and thumb by rolling the skin over them.

The most common symptom is a lump of any size but you should book an appointment with your GP if you have any new feelings in the scrotal area.

On a lighter note, most lumps in the scrotum aren't cancer, and if it does turn out to be cancer, it's one of the most treatable forms of the disease. You should get to know your balls like the back of your hand.

Maintaining an erection

Erectile dysfunction, or impotence, is unfortunately common from middle age onwards and it's caused by a narrowing of the blood vessels that pump blood to create and maintain an erection.

This narrowing may occur for a number of reasons but high blood pressure, diabetes and smoking are high on the list. Giving up smoking seems like a no-brainer, and maintaining a healthy body weight and undertaking regular exercise reduce your risk of developing high blood pressure and diabetes.

Protect your cock from STIs

STIs are invisible and often give no symptoms for many years so you won't know if you've just passed one on, so you should always wear a condom. Available free at GPs and sexual health clinics, they significantly reduce the risk of the transmission of STIs but they're nowhere near as effective if they remain unopened in your wallet.

There are so many easy ways to get tested for STIs - a simple fingerpick test can detect HIV, and many GP surgeries have urine pots to test for chlamydia and gonorrhoea that you can pick up and drop off discretely without even making an appointment. No excuses.

Be careful with trimming

Many of us take pleasure in keeping neat and tidy. There are no hard and fast rules about what to do here, but a sensible one is to exercise caution.

Be especially careful in the craggy terrain of your scrotum if shaving, where it can be technically more challenging to not make a tiny cut in the skin - this could potentially introduce harmful bacteria which could cause cellulitis, abscesses or worse, Fournier's gangrene (Googling not recommended).

Penis size really doesn't matter to women

A 2015 survey of women presented with photographs of all types and sizes of cocks published in the Journal of Sexual Medicine revealed that penis length was one of the least valued attributes. "Overall cosmetic appearance" came out on top. So no need to worry about whether your cock size is above or below average. Just keep it looking good.

Use your penis to keep it healthy

Make ejaculation part of your daily routine. Here's why: a large Harvard study of nearly 30,000 men found the risk of prostate cancer was 33 per cent lower in men who'd ejaculated at least 21 times per month, compared to those who ejaculated only 4-7 times per month. This included ejaculations during sex, masturbation and, um, "nocturnal emissions". Time to play catch up.

Lasting Longer and Harder

Have you ever suffered from bouts of erectile dysfunction or premature ejaculation (especially when it mattered the most to you to perform well)?

It's completely normal. It's also completely avoidable. And it can be so much better.

Want to turn your sex life from something that gives you anxiety into something that you confidently crave? Want to know that you can be up for the challenge whenever it presents itself? Want to know that you will forever be able to sexually provide for your partner?

No more having to rely on excuses like "Sorry, I guess I had too much to drink", "I'm just not in the mood tonight", or "I came that quickly because you just looked so damn sexy".

It's time to strengthen your cock for better sex, firmer erections, and legendary lasting power between the sheets.

Before I get into the specific action steps that you can start using today to strengthen your penis for better sex, you might be wondering... is it even possible?

Q - Is It Possible To Strengthen Your cock?
A - Absolutely, yes, it is possible to strengthen your penis.

Depending on your unique genetic make up, your cock is made up of anywhere from 30-60% what is known as smooth muscle tissue. And just like other kinds of muscle tissue, it can grow (or shrink) depending on how you use it....

Sharpen Your Own Sword
It's never been easier to acquire over the counter quick-fixes for semi-occasional erectile dysfunction. But avoid the temptation!

Not only will you not strengthen your penis naturally... these pills/herbs/supplements only make the problem worse- on multiple levels.

Mentally, the products may make you feel confident for a brief period of time, but they'll make you feel worse about yourself and your ability to perform in the long-term because you will have used a crutch. You won't be building authentic confidence because the performance won't have come from you, but from the product.

On the physical level, pills and supplements have a tendency to make you so (sometimes painfully) hard that you actually lose temporary sensation in your penis to a large extent.

I can't attest to this personally but I have had over a dozen clients complain that the pills actually made them so hard that it hurt them so badly that they had to use ice packs to make their erections go down. So stay away

CHAPTER FIVE

HOW TO VALUE YOU, EVEN MORE

Your relationship might be going great but you feel that it is time to take things a notch above. The only problem is that you don't really know how to make your woman want you more. Read on to find out what to and what not to do to keep a guy hooked and wanting more!

Retain your independence

Just because you have a girlfriend does not mean that you will relegate your life to her service. Make your girl a part of your life and not everything that's in it. You keep your independence, make your own money and hang out with your set of friends and make time for her and you will see how much she values you.

Don't cramp her space

Girls like their space and they do not want any man around when they are having their girl time or bonding time. Even if your girl says that it's OK for you to come out on girl's night, decline the offer and encourage her to go alone and honestly be fine with it. Your girl will love you for it!

Don't hound her

Don't be her satellite and hound her 24/7 trying to find out where she is or what she is doing. Do this and you will bore her soon enough. Give her some time off and let her be. Your girl will surely call you more often if you don't give her grief for forgetting to call when she had said she would or for calling late.

Don't push her

Don't push her to do things against her will. If she does not want to hang out with your set of malefriends then bail her out. Bend the rules a little and if you feel that she has to make an appearance at a do with you then give her the option of leaving after a little while.

Do fun things

Make her see the relaxed and fun side of you by doing some crazy stuff together. Go bungee jumping or have an all you can drink night and show her how much of unadulterated fun she can have with you!

Never compare

Never make the mistake of comparing your relationship with others. Any form of comparison whether materialistic or emotional will make you look immature and will put him off instantly. Be happy with what you have and make him feel the happiness that he brings to you. Your feeling will be reciprocated and he will want you even more.

Create More Satisfaction Every Day

Want to know how your values can create more satisfaction and joy in your life every day? Upfront it's quite simple, clarify your core values and make daily choices that are in alignment with them.

Unfortunately most of us face a different reality - we're so busy working, parenting and living that we're living a life which is more "just in time" instead of conscious and connected to our core.

Here's an analogy I like to use to help individuals just like you become aware of what it means to be more conscious of your core and core values.

Put your finger at the tip of your nose now. The tip of your nose is the part that starts to curve under. Guess what although you can see most of your finger, you can't see where the tip of your nose meets the tip of your finger.

Although you know you have a "tip" on your nose you're not aware of what's happening there because it's out of your immediate sight. This is how most of us live every day - simply living your day without full awareness.

Now move the end of your finger up just a little bit and you'll be able to see it because now it's physically in front of you. If you're like 98% of the population you pay much more attention to what's visually in front of you.

Although the tip of your nose is always there, just like your core values are a part of who you are, when you are not consciously making choices that are in alignment with them you are not taking action that is fully supportive of you creates a level of satisfaction and joy that continues to get you out of bed in the morning ready and excited to begin your day.

You'll also notice that if you're not conscious of your core value that you probably tend to procrastinate when it comes to both your daily and long term goals.

The truth is, when you can't physically see something it's easy not to pay attention to it because although it seems like we should know what our core values are, most of us don't take time on a daily basis or even an annual basis to reconnect to them.

Instead you may have made an assumption that your core values from oh a decade or so ago are the same ones that are most important to you right now. Guess what, change is constant, what that means to you is that your core values are also shifting in level of importance.

I've worked with hundreds of individuals who prior to our partnership spend more time creating a fun dinner with friends then they do focusing on what's at the core of their foundation often because they "think" they know.

What they immediately learn is that some of what they said is most important is outdated or really the opinion of someone else, and they're not taking consistent action to support what is important. You can tell if this is you if you complain about things in your life.

Don't worry if you keep reading you'll learn a few things to help you get reconnected to what's most important.

Right now jot down your three most important core values. The mere action of doing this brings them into your current awareness. Now ask yourself, are these three values what I really think is most important or what I think should be most important.

If it's the later do it again. Next to each value write down "why" it's your core value. What you're looking for is your emotional reason for the core value you choose. This emotional why is what makes your core value come alive to you.

For example someone may choose "family" because their emotional why is "connection and adventure" and you may choose it because it's about "feeling taken care of and love" - for each person this is true.

Let's pretend you choose family, health and inner harmony as your top three core values. By making this choice you've just moved your finger from the tip of your nose where you can't see it, into your vision and consciousness.

When you become conscious you become more and more aware of your true self; what's really important on a daily basis. It makes it easy to make choices that support you and fill you with more of your "emotional why".

Again, knowing your core values provides you criteria so that you are more aware of both what you don't want, and more importantly what you do want more of in your daily life.

When you understand these distinctions you are able to more consciously stop complaining about what you can't control and do and take actions that support and create more of what supports your core values.

The Secrets of A Long Lasting Romance

Trust me, the infatuation you feel as a result of a budding romance will not last very long. But if you really value the person you met from a free dating website, you can transform your relationship from a craze-driven feeling to a deep, dependable love that will last you a lifetime.

It is foolish to assume that love does not require hard work from the couple. You should always strive to make your partner feel loved and valued every time.

Here are some tips to make that special someone you found on a free dating site will feel your love to the fullest.

Initiate Open Communication

Sit down with your partner and calmly discuss the things that you like and do not like about the relationship. Be open-minded about your partner's views and try to reach a compromise.

If you can talk anything out, it will be easier for you to understand how each other tick. Being able to communicate openly with each other will positively impact your relationship.

This is one way of furthering your relationship with the partner you found on a free dating site.

Continue to Develop Intimacy

It is always a red flag when couples stop touching or saying affectionate things to each other. Physical and emotional intimacy is important in a relationship.

When things get serious with the person you met on a free dating website, kissing or hugging that person when he or she least expects it is one way of being intimate.

Spice things up in the bedroom. But most importantly, make your partner feel appreciated by constantly assuring him or her with affectionate words.

Spend Some Time Together.

As things progress with the person you met through a free online dating site, find activities that you both enjoy then do it as often as you can.

From time to time, break away from your regular date nights and do something new. It can be as simple as going to a new restaurant or as crazy as a bungee jumping weekend. Sharing new experiences together helps solidify your relationship.

Spend Some Time Apart from Each Other

It is also important to spend some time apart from your partner that you met through a free dating site so you won't get tired of each other. Familiarity breeds contempt, they say. So if you are a guy, let her have her all girls night out once a week.

For women, allow your man to go bowling or play fantasy football with his friends. You should put your complete trust on your partner so that means no interrogation after he or she had her solo time.

Treat Each Other as Equal

Never feel superior because you earn more or you think you are smarter. If you do that, your partner that you met via free online dating website will resent it and your relationship will become a fight for power.

You should understand that each of you compensate for each other's weaknesses. When it comes to big decisions, plan and decide on them together.

Start Over With a Clean Slate

If the relationship with a partner you found on a dating site starts to get rocky, encourage him or her to start over.

Don't bring up past mistakes when you are having an argument. Learn to let go of ancient hurts and resentments if you want to save your relationship. Starting over gives you a chance to rekindle a romance that you think both of you have lost.

CHAPTER SIX

FINDING YOUR POWER AND COURAGE OUT OF THE ASHES - PART 1

Alpha Male Power transforms you into a powerful, supremely confident alpha male. It eliminates all fear, nervousness and anxiety related to women and socializing. It allows you to instinctively attract women on the deepest level possible.

Alpha Male Power is about tapping into the infinite power of your inner alpha male, which then allows you to approach women at will (and without any fear) and attract women on a deep and instinctive level.

Women are more attracted to alpha males than any other type of male, so all you need to do is say and do a few simple things that trigger her natural attraction to alpha males and she will be immediately interested in you.

The techniques in this program also cause other men to feel a constant, overwhelming need to respect you and want to be friendly towards you. Guys avoid messing with you because they know that you're someone they should respect and be nice to.

The only guaranteed CURE for approach anxiety: Many guys waste years of their life being too afraid to walk up and talk to women they find attractive.

No matter how much they pump themselves up or how much they learn about "pick up," they just can't seem to stop feeling anxious and nervous when it comes time to approach a woman they find attractive.

If you experience approach anxiety, get ready to say GOOD-BYE to it forever. We have found the CURE! From now on, your approach anxiety will literally CEASE TO EXIST. Prepare to experience a life completely free of anxiety and unnecessary nervousness.

Ultimate alpha male mindset

These powerful mindsets will change the way you view your own personal power from now on. No longer will you experience periods of weakness, self-doubt or insecurity. You will feel powerful, unstoppable and always able to take on anything, no matter how challenging.

As a side bonus, women can SENSE when a man has these mindsets and it is DEEPLY attractive to them on the most primal of levels. Other guys will pale in comparison to what she feels for you.

Making women like you automatically

Imagine if the next time you spoke to a woman she liked you AUTOMATICALLY. Meaning, you did NOT have to try to get her to like you. This is not only possible, it is NORMAL and a small percentage of men around the world know how to do it.

You can have this type of power over women. Just use the techniques in this program and you will experience it IMMEDI-ATELY. Say goodbye to trying to pick women up or hoping that they like you. From now on, women will like you automatically.

Overcoming your "inner game" issues with women: Know-ing what to say is important, but a woman can TELL if you are nervous or anxious when talking to her and it turns her OFF at a deep level. Women don't want to feel like they are more powerful than you.

Fixing your inner game/confidence issues with women is CRITICAL if you want to enjoy the success you've been dreaming about. In this program, you will discover how to instantly and painlessly eliminate all of your issues with women. From now on, you will experience a life of confidence, self-esteem, power and control. No more insecurities, no more nervousness, no more fear.

Constant confidence

Do you feel confident in some situations, but really nervous and unsure of yourself in others? Get ready to experience life with unwavering confidence that NEVER goes away. You will have to experience it to believe it because we are well aware that it sounds "too good to be true." Try it and you will see.

Powerful presence

Your presence and vibe is one of the top two most important things for success with women. If you're vibe is off or you are "all in your head" because of nervousness or anxiety, women simply won't be able to feel proper (if any) attraction for you.

Having sex with a LOT of women

A lot of guys dream of being able to "get laid" with a new woman every week, or even a few women every week. Yet, the closest most guys ever come to that is by watching porn.

The fact is, there is a small percentage of men in the world who do most of the sexing of the available women. Discover a SURPRISING way of interacting with women that causes them to want to have sex with you IMMEDIATELY.

To say that you will be AMAZED by the reactions you get from women when you use this technique is an understatement. This is going to change your life BIG TIME.

Attracting very beautiful women

Why do so many ordinary and "ugly" looking men have very attractive girlfriends? What is going on there? Any guy can attractive very beautiful women, but most guys simply don't know what to do.

Respected by other alpha males

If other strong men don't respect you, then you will often be the butt of their jokes, will be overlooked for many promotions in work environments and most importantly – you will be overlooked by women.

When women see that you an alpha male who is respected by other strong men, they will feel attraction for you on a level that they simply cannot experience for weaker men.

Being a powerful man

A lot of men are afraid of their true potential and shy away from positions of power and responsibility. When it comes to talking to women, many men would rather hand over their power to a woman in the hope that she will choose them and give them a chance to have sex with her.

Yet, that is not how an alpha male behaves and it is NOT what a woman wants. Women are attracted to men who rise up (even slightly or momentarily) into positions of power. Don't shy away from being the powerful man you know that you can be.

Maximum masculinity

The fact is, the more masculine you are, the more attractive you are to women. A lot of modern men have been turned into "half men, half women" by pop culture and have suppressed much of their masculinity in a confused attempt to impress women.

Women are NOT impressed by men who drop their rank and place the woman as the alpha. Women are impressed by MEN and PREFER men to be in the top position.

Making friends with the "cool crowd": Some guys find it difficult to relate and get along with the "cool crowd," especially if there are a number of alpha males or very attractive women in the group.

Deepest level of confidence

Confidence is not finite. Your confidence can grow, build and increase as time goes on. However, most guys will only ever experience a superficial level of confidence, confidence in some situations or fleeting/temporary confidence during good times.

Using your alpha male power

Once you know what this elusive and highly-prized power is, how do you use it? Discover how to use your natural, alpha male power to change your life (and the world if you want to) for the better. Your alpha male power will make women submit to you, make other men respect you and make you feel like a king.

Alpha male behavior

Learn the many important behaviors that are critical to being a true alpha male. Find out the many mistakes that men make, which place them below alpha males and cause them to live the life of a lower ranking male.

Being a "good guy" alpha male

Some men use their position as the alpha male in a bad way, to hurt, harm or hinder others. Yet, if you're reading this right now – you're probably not a bad guy with bad intentions with women and the world.

Most guys who arrive at The Modern Man site are good guys who want more success with women and more respect from others in general. In this program, you'll learn how to maintain the good guy part of yourself while also rising up to become the alpha who others follow and whom women lust after.

Mojo for life

Discover how to tap into an endless source of motivation, drive, determination and passion unlike anything you have ever experienced before. This section is quite "deep and meaningful", but also simple and practical at the same time.

From now on, you will feel like you can take on the world and will be full of confidence, drive and mojo for life. Nothing will bring you down, nothing will make you feel insecure and nothing will stop you from getting what you truly want with women and in life.

Being alpha around women

A lot of modern women behave as though they are alpha females, but in reality it's just a test to see if you'll fold and hand over your power.

In this program, you'll discover many things to say and do around women to show them that you are a true alpha. You will also learn how to be a true alpha because women can spot a fake and when they do, they lose interest immediately.

Avoiding bullying/being picked on

Bullies, bad men and mean people are ATTRACTED to weaker people as their victims.

If you don't display alpha male behavior and psychology and place yourself below other men in terms of rank, you will invite these people to pick on you, cause problems for you and harm you to make help feel good about themselves.

Attracting women on the deepest level

Most modern men don't understand what REALLY attracts women, so they get caught up in what they see in TV advertisements, magazines and movies. They assume that if they wear a nice shirt, build some muscle and have a nice hairstyle, they will then be attractive to women. Yet, that is only SUPERFICIAL attraction.

The most powerful type of attraction is what a woman feels DEEP down; her primal, instinctive attraction. In this program, you will learn EXACTLY how to trigger a woman's deep, instinctive attraction for you no matter what you look like, what race you are or what you do for a living.

You will have to experience it to believe it, but when you do

– you will smile because you will KNOW that your life will never be the same again. Suddenly, you will have the power to attract basically any woman you meet.

No more fear

Most men experience some level of fear when it comes to women, some more than others. However, as a true alpha male, you WILL NOT experience fear around women.

Whether you are approaching a woman for the first time, in the middle of a conversation, escalating to sex or in the middle of having sex with her – you will NEVER experience fear. Instead, you will powerful, confident and calmly in charge and women will LIKE that.

Being alpha during sex

There's nothing sexier for a woman to be with a man who is truly THERE when he is sexing her. If you're afraid to embrace your alpha position, you will never sex her in the way that she truly desires.

CHAPTER SEVEN

Our society's becoming emasculated. Our men are becoming soft, weak, and vain.

If you're offended by that statement then I'm likely talking to you. If you agree with it, if you see that the tides are turning for the worse, then I'm likely not.

If you're doing any of the things on this list, don't get your panties in a knot, just stop doing them.

Our society was literally built by the hands of strong men who did the work without complaint. It's being destroyed by men who don't know how to be men. Boys who aspire for fame above all else at incredible numbers.

Males who aren't concerned about winning or losing, rather, about popularity, about finding themselves, about getting what they feel they deserve without doing the work to get it.

1. Stop taking selfies

It's weird. It's vain. Its not that there is anything wrong with selfies but the intention behind taking a selfie. Especially the dangerous selfies

2. Stop thinking you're entitled to a single thing

You're not entitled to someone else's money. You're not entitled to a job. You're not entitled to happiness, only its pursuit.

3. Stop complaining

Men don't complain. They don't cry about how things are, they accept them and do what they need to do to make them better.

4. Stop comparing yourself to others

Social media has made this the norm. Stop it. Stop wishing you were in someone else's shoes. Stop wanting what someone else has. Stop looking over the fence and start looking in the mirror.

5. Stop watching porn

It makes you unable to have boners as, over time, your expectations change. It changes how you treat women, for the worse. It changes what you want from women. It changes your ideas of what sex is and should be.

Go get a real woman, treat her well and with respect, and poke all you want. But stop with the porn, it's turning a generation into impotent, sadistic cowards who treat women like objects. (Read This: Does Porn Have a Place in a Man's Life?)

6. Stop watching TV

Read a book instead.

7. Stop worrying about your clothes

Clothes don't make the man. Take pride in how you present yourself, sure, but stop fretting over your appearance, thinking that appearance is the measure of a man. The content of your character is who you are and who you are to the rest of humanity. The clothes you wear mean fuck all.

8. Stop being a little bitch

Stop hiding behind this idea that there is no right or wrong. Stand up for what's right. Fight what's wrong. Stop being a little bitch and take a stance. Fight for those who can't fight for themselves.

9. Stop letting your fear inhibit my freedom

Stop trying to take my guns. Stop trying to tell me what gun I can and can't buy. If you don't want to defend yourself or your family, if you'd rather have help be a phone call away rather than by your bed, so be it. But don't let your fear inhibit my freedom. Don't be a pussy.

10. Stop thinking you know everything

We dig our heels in now more than ever. We take a stance and we have no real idea why the stance is taken. Every single human on this planet knows something that you don't and has something to teach you. Go into every conversation with humility, not like you're the professor and class is in session.

11. Stop blaming other people and entities for your lack of anything

This life is on you. Whether you're happy, of value, and successful is on you. It isn't the result of anything other than your own choices and actions. Stop blaming others for your lack of anything. Start taking control of your life, your thoughts, and your choices or just shut up.

12. Stop waiting for the perfect job to come your way, take the next one available

Too many humans think they're destined for something perfect when they haven't earned it. They're too good to do this, they're above that. The reality is that you need a bloody paycheck, so take the next job and work your ass off, climb the ladder, be better than your wage, and reap the future rewards.

13. Stop being a dick

Smile. Be kind. Be good. Complement people. Help people. Open doors for women. Give your time to something other than your own benefit. Stop being an entitled prick, start being the good man you're capable of being.

14. Stop being insecure

Stop being so insecure that you can't rejoice in the success of others. Stop being so insecure that you can't be kind to your fellow man. Know that you're better than the insecure prick who needs to push others down to feel good about himself.

15. Stop being a bully

Strength is given not to punish but to uplift. Fight for others, don't pick on them. Defend others, don't make fun of them. If you're strong you have the chance to lead. If you're a bully you're going to get your ass kicked one of these days, if not by another human, by life as you end yours alone and without true, valuable relationships.

16. Stop sleeping in

Stop being lazy. It isn't your right to be lazy. That's not freedom. Freedom is earned, it's won, it's appreciated. When someone else is taking care of you, you have no freedom.

17. Stop waiting

Start acting. Start chasing your goals, your dreams, and hunting down your fears. Stop waiting for a gift, a promotion, a helping hand, go out and get it. It may take years to get what you want, but persist. God didn't make you a quitter.

18. Stop quitting

Stop quitting when things get tough. Tribulation is opportunity, it always is and always has been. When the economy tanks, those who've saved their money, who've stayed disciplined when things were going well will have the chance to cash in.

When the shit hits the fan you're given an opportunity to persist, to push through, to become tougher and stronger. Stop quitting when it's easier to quit, keep pushing.

19. Stop pouting

Life can suck. It's harsh. It isn't easy. Bad shit happens to good people all the time. But pouting is useless. CHOOSE to look at the bright side, to appreciate wherever you are and the opportunities you have.

20. Stop wasting your money

Spend money on experiences and other people, not on things, nor on yourself. Money can be a great thing. It can help others. It can open your eyes to new ways of living, different cultures, climates, and creations. Stop wasting it on stupid shit. Start using it to enrich your life and the lives of others.

21. Stop gossiping

Gossip is weak, yet it dominates conversations. Men don't do that shit. Talk about ideas, not other people. If you enter a conversation and it turns to gossip, excuse yourself from the conversation. Be better than that. Be about more than that.

Like it or not, the world that we live in has become way too over effeminate. Obviously, it's bound to get a man get down on himself. Feeling down right low is different, but having to get down within the dating marketing place is a whole other depressive story, right men?

Be it stupid rituals, or pointless fashion, hoop jumping, political correctness, an existence that is approved only by an 8-to-6-corporate-PR or perhaps even so-called modern-day politeness - it looks as if the world at times focuses on getting us men down!

But, You Are Alpha Male Stock, So Buck Up!

Give it a logical thought, get those brain juices flowing, let your Alpha male lineage take over, because you need to acknowledge that you descend from a long line of Alpha males. These were extraordinary, action oriented men, who were leaders, who were at the top of their pack.

Back in the days, no one but the Alpha males had the right to breed; it was them that ruled. It's just been the last couple thousands of years that all these social norms and marriage issues have come into existence in order to even things out a bit, however, all the millions of years before them, it was you, the alpha male that was produced by the smartest and the strongest of the pack.

Well, of course, that doesn't leave out the fact that there might have been a few, sneaky and slimy betas around that might have sneaked their ways into the pants of all those ladies, but well, there are always exceptions in life.

They were nothing but a minority; whereas you are the descendant of the strongest, meanest, nastiest and most powerful 'bad asses' of the times! Every single one of them, all those ultimate Alpha males succeeded in evolutionary battles. That yucky beta male genes, those followers, they just got dropped down along the sides; those nasty pigs!

The Alpha Male Dating Life

If you've been blaming your genes for your bad, unhappy and unsatisfactory dating life, you have got to stop right away! Never, I repeat, you must never utter things like "I'm too short", "I'm too tall", "I'm too ugly", "I'm too simple", "I'm too whatever". Think of this, did all these physiological aspects stop your daring and powerful ancestors? It didn't, right? So, why should it stop you? It shouldn't!

There would always remain the fact that you have received your genes from only the best. They come from only the most action oriented, most worthy and go getting Alpha males! Give your history a good luck and you would get an amazing past filled with more than 6.5 million years of success with the best, the most beautiful and sinfully gorgeous women!

No matter how bad things get, there's just no overlooking the fact that however adverse or terrifying the entire dating situation got, every single ancestor of yours fought the odds and overcame them - they didn't give up, they didn't play the blame game.

Every single element of your being is ingrained with these alpha male qualities - there's no running away from it, there's no helping it, so don't even try to make an escape!

Let the animal inside you take over

Yes, that's true. Deep inside, you are nothing but an animal. That too, an animal that is built and meant to breed. And if you have any doubts about having been built for it, God are you wrong or what! Believe it - you are built to perfection for breeding! That's what you're supposed to do!

Don't Let the Civil Society Numb You Down!

The civil society is making and will continue to make horrid attempts to numb you down. Rather than going to battle, you are made to go to football games, where you just get to scream and shout - where did smelling the turf go?

Rather than hunting packs we get to sit cornered in the corporate world, slaving away on computers and files with our wives giving us head once a month as if it's a mere ritual! But, dear fellow Alpha males; do not lose faith.

Even if our battle field has changed, even if we are more enclosed, we need to be understanding, intelligent and courageous. If you numb down, you will be disrespecting your amazing lineage, you will be disappointing our strong and powerful alpha male history! Instead of just getting lost in this outrageous world, be brave - be the Alpha male that you truly are meant to be!

And while you are at it, don't you dare blame your genes - they are meant to succeed!

CHAPTER EIGHT

HOW TO REFRAME ANY CHALLENGE
INTO YOUR OPPORTUNITY TO GET
MUCH, MUCH STRONGER

Overcome anger by using a simple but powerful happiness technique... it will can make you happier, healthier and more successful. The key to success is using your mind more creatively and strategically.

Knowing how to turn a bad situation into a good one can make the difference between success and failure, or happiness and unhappiness. If you perceive any negative situation in beneficial ways you'll feel more confident in dealing with it.

Reframing
Reframing a bad situation in a favorable way will give you the power to overcome anger and lower depression, while boosting your morale.

And it will help you to find the silver lining in every cloud.
Reframing, a powerful happiness technique, is one of the most important skills used by optimists to keep the upper hand, lower depression or avoid getting depressed. And... this is one of the favorite techniques used by my clients to increase their optimistic thinking. Once they get the hang of it, they love it.

Reframing simply involves taking a negative situation and turning it around in your mind in a way that makes it appear more positive.

Reframing let's you uncover the hidden positive aspects of a dark situation or event, and gives you a sense of control over a difficult situation... and helps you to overcome anger and frustration.

Case Example

Let's say you have a new supervisor at your job...

And your co-worker forms a negative opinion of the person, which influences you to take a critical view, as well. Your co-worker thinks the new boss is terrible, and feels she'll hate working under her. Do you have to give in to the prevailing pessimistic view?

You can counter this negative assumption by developing a more hopeful narrative. You can find something you like about the supervisor, and tell yourself a different story.

First, you can give her a chance... and second you can try to form a positive impression... and third you can seek to build a good relationship with her.

Your optimistic approach with enable you to feel good about the future, and enhance your chances of working well with the new supervisor. You'll feel less depressed and anxious. You'll be less prone to become angry every time something happens in the office.

Why don't you get some practice reframing? You'll soon be able to reframe even the worst situation. Reframing won't make a bad situation go away, but it will help you to survive and often to conquer it.

Situation:

It's raining out, but you wanted to play tennis. How can you reframe it?

Possible reframe: Instead of getting down, why not find something to do indoors... something you've been wanting to find time to do?

Situation: You go to the doctor and find out you have an incurable disease.

Possible reframe: Rather than giving in to panic and despair, you could read everything on the disease you can find and try to identify ways to keep the disease from getting worse. You'll overcome anger and tap into the natural healing power of optimism.

Try to find good reframes for other problems or events in your life. Be creative and let your imagination loose!

See Problems As Opportunities In Disguise

Believe it or not, problems can actually make you happier. How? Let's think of it this way...

Each problem is a hidden opportunity to reframe and reinvent a situation constructively. It's a challenge, but it can be done. And, by solving one problem at a time, or facing the challenge therein, you'll gain confidence and strength... which will make you more resilient.

Reframing unfortunate circumstances will give you a sense of accomplishment. You'll grow as you deal with the challenges of your life, and you'll have fun turning each challenge to your advantage. Plus, creative reframing is another way to cultivate optimism... and if you cultivate optimism...

Lifelong happiness will be yours!

The recent research on happiness reveals just how effective optimism is in giving people greater happiness. it will make you happier and more prosperous.

Let's Summarize

Try a simple happiness technique and success strategy called reframing to help you overcome anger and decrease depression. And see if you don't feel less fearful, anxious or depressed... and more in control of your life.

Even if you aren't depressed or angry, optimism can keep you from getting that way. Remember to find the good in a bad event and turn it to your advantage by strategically reframing it along more hopeful lines.

Refaming and other optimistic skills will make you happier and healthier, and give you more joy and pleasure in your life.

Can We Reframe The Problem?

Overcoming Objections will always be at the heart of every sales encounter. Although the laws that govern human psychology and motivation never change, the same cannot be said for the ever-evolving objection-handling techniques that now require far more sophistication to satisfy the needs of today's customer.

A quick look in the rearview mirror clearly demonstrates that at times, even the experts, sometimes get it wrong!

In the 1960s and early 70s, selling courses like PSSI [Professional Selling Skills / Level I] taught us to "Ignore the 'First' objection".

The logic was, 'at the beginning of a sales encounter, most customers will put out an objection - any objection - even if it isn't valid, in order to provide themselves a certain feeling of control'. To dwell too much on the first objection was deemed by PSSI experts to be, time and effort, spent unproductively.

The fact is, it didn't take long - less than a decade - for sales people to see the folly in this approach. That, in tandem with more knowledgeable buyers and more complex products/solutions, changes to this strategy was essential.

The good new is that today, much of Carnegie's strategy is as valid an approach as it was several decades ago; in keeping with the basic mantra of successful selling, "Find out what they want...

then... Give it to them!" That is, with one caveat, find out what they want First!

If this was all there was to objection-handling, though, every salesperson would be successful. Clearly, there is more to it than that.

For example, what is the answer to a customer that says, "We are not in the market! ... We have no budget.

At this point, unsuccessful sellers get busy folding their metaphorical tents to make a hasty retreat because they find themselves bereft of a deeper understanding or skill-set required to overcome a sales-ending objection - ironically, before the selling process can even take place.

What is meant by this?
Simply, those of us, who have taken Social PSYC in university or college, understand that 'to the degree a person articulates their position [bad or good] makes the chances of changing their mind, exponentially more difficult than it is if they never said a thing'.

Psychologically, people want to save face, they don't want to be manipulated or sold and therefore, quite naturally, dig their heels in once they have stated their position.

I am reminded of the expression, "A man convinced against his will... is of the same opinion still!"

Good sellers know this and they know other important things too, like:

1) There are ways to address objections like these, and
2) They must be handled delicately and professionally.

To better understand the mind of an elite seller, it is best to reflect on how salespeople process information like, for example: "We have no budget!"

Unsuccessful sellers interpret this as 'there is no money, no where, no how' - and then conduct themselves accordingly.

Elite sellers, however, begin asking themselves, "What does the customer mean by no budget? Was there a budget that has been spent? Is there a budget that has been frozen? Will there be another budget - if so when?" etc.

The point here is,

1) The seller has not forgotten the need his/her product may satisfy, and

2) They understand that "We have no budget!" can have many meanings - each of which, with an opportunity to continue negotiations, albeit with one important fact, the customer must be allowed to Save Face.

1) Repeat the objection "You have no budget at this time" - which accomplishes two important, psychological steps:

a) The customer hears that the seller has heard and understood his/her objection [very critical] and,

b) "...at this time" - diminishes or lessons the objection thereby eliminating the Full-Stop scenario bringing the potential to go forward, back into play.

2) The second and perhaps the most important step is to openly 'Validate' the objection. Simply, agree that the customer's objection is a valid objection - one with which you can sincerely empathize and agree with as being a challenge - in your mind, though, not a sales ender.

You could say something like, "Not having a budget at this time is a challenge and I don't blame you for feeling the way you do [or words to that effect].

Note: By validating and agreeing with the concerns of the customer, we seem more sincere and trustworthy - which we are -

allowing the essential Buyer-Seller bonding process to cultivate, especially since we both now, appear to have concerns in common.

Having accomplished all of this, the elite seller may say something like: "Can we perhaps, Mr/Ms Customer, reframe the problem?" or "Maybe if we look at reframing this budgetary dilemma in a different way, we may find an alternative solution." or "Mr/Ms Customer, sometimes when I step back and reframe a challenge, I often find positive alternatives I've overlooked."

One could go on but the important point here is, having bonded with the customer, having validated and minimized [in this case] the budgetary concern, we have allowed the customer to save face on his/her original sale-ending position, that in turn opens up a new positive dialogue with the express purpose of finding ways to overcome the objection - and there are many!

Financing may be an alternative. Split [corporate, inter-departmental, inter-budgetary] billing, renting, rent-to-own, rent-to-new-budget, conditional purchase financial installments, et al. Without a doubt, there are alternatives to a Full-Stop scenario. I personally live by the credo, "Where there is a will... there is a Relative!" Elite sellers look to solutions - not obstacles.

The Bottom Line: Objection-Handling is both an art and a science, requiring understanding, proficiency and practice. The goal is to instill a sense of empathy and sincerity for the challenges faced by our customers with an undaunted focus to allowing buyers to change their mind, whilst saving face.

CHAPTER NINE

HOW TO CREATE ACCOUNTABILITY IN YOUR LIFE SO YOU DON'T LOSE

These tactics of maintaining unclear relationships and prolonging break-ups all produce what I call stable ambiguity; too afraid to be alone, but unwilling to fully engage in intimacy building—a holding pattern that affirms the undefined nature of the relationship, which has a mix of comforting consistency AND the freedom of blurred lines.

We want to have our cake and eat it too. We want to have someone available to cozy-up with when it's snowing, but if something better comes along, we want the freedom to explore.

In this relationship culture, expectations and trust are in constant question. The state of stable ambiguity inevitably creates an atmosphere where at least one person feels lingering uncertainty, and neither person feels truly appreciated or nurtured. We do this at the expense of our emotional health, and the emotional health of others.

How many adults do you know? What exactly is an adult? My light-hearted and serious response when asked about adults? -"Don't let the big bodies fool you!" Adults are neither as common as you might naively assume, nor as rare as you might reasonably expect.

That doesn't mean there are all that many out there, and what do I know? Look in the Webster's New World Dictionary, Third College Edition and find "adult" defined as "grown up" and "mature in age, size, strength, etc."

Then, look up the word "mature" in the same source and find "fully developed, as a person, a mind, etc." Seems rather circular, doesn't it? Does anyone really know what is being described? What are we even talking about?

It's also easy to come across a slew of quotes that ennoble children and ridicule adults. Is all this just so-called grown ups being envious of and yearning for the joyful, carefree playfulness of youth and employing self-depreciatory humor cheaply aimed at adult's mundane responsibilities and muted affect?

Consider another view, like the above quote by misanthropist Ambrose Bierce, which skewers adults as chronically blaming others and call it a day, instead of owning total responsibility for their own lives.

Just look at what adults actually do. Adults usually do engage in gainful employment on a regular basis, take care of their self-, partner-, family- and extended family-care.

Adults are answerable for their life obligations, including employment, bill paying, house chores and upkeep, and being as good as their word. Adults are held responsible for what they sign up to do in both their public and private lives, such as what they say, write, promise and do.

Adults are held accountable for their actions and commitments in life, whether that is in a relationship, marriage or friendship, in a work environment with meeting both the letter and spirit of their job description, and in the community being a worthwhile citizen in regard to keeping their house and yard kept up, being informed of community issues and welfare in addition to political candidates and public issues, and regularly participating in the voting process.

When you watch what adults do, this does have a ring of maturity in being full developed as a person. Actually being an adult in all these ways is rather a high watermark to meet for almost all of us.

So you might ask, what's so hard being an adult after all? Well, to state the obvious, it isn't one bit bloody easy, and hardly getting easier with all the modern times in the Western world brings in terms of diversions, distractions, entertainments, mobile devices, gaming platforms/games, internet, speed of life, governmental regulation, dealing with bureaucracies and stupidities, and the exponentially increasing stuff of life to somehow fit in the same 24 hours a day, 168 hours a week, just like everyone else.

Who has the time? Who has the passionate fire in the belly? Is it all to run faster away from all the ego-mind's saber-rattling fears, ultimately of death, nothingness and annihilation, or is it all to run faster toward all the ego-mind's dreamed up selfish gratifications, greedy attachments and wants media-manipulated into supposed needs?

It's like being caught in a vice, a stranglehold, somewhere between a rock and a hard spot, all orchestrated and choreographed courtesy of one imaginary self or ego-mind.

It is proposed that self-responsibility or self-accountability is the quintessential defining attribute to qualify as an adult. The word responsibility literally means "response-ability," that is, possessing the ability to respond.

So self-responsibility means to not only have the ability to respond, decide and choose, but further to participate in an engaged, most practical possible fashion in taking responsibility for your entire life.

See the attribute of being responsible for oneself as at once having the capacity, the willingness and actually enacting in the behavior (sometimes called "praxis") of living moment to moment.

Self-responsibility can be seen in taking care of doing what you said, promised and signed up to do, without any if's, but's, blaming others, rationalizations, reasons, or sniveling excuses for not doing what there is to do, as long as there's some way within the parameters of reality to honorably do it.

This character trait of self-responsibility is synonymous with self-accountability. In a like fashion, accountability literally means "account-ability," that is, owning the ability to account for your own life.

To be self-accountable means to be answerable for the obligations and duties you have in your life by the very nature of being a live human being in the web of life on planet Earth.

Any one who is self-accountable answers fundamentally to him- or herself in honoring a code of living, ethics and integrity that goes to the depth of who every one of us actually is, on the highest, deepest and broadest of levels, and ultimately on the indwelling and transcendent Divine realm.

It's actually pretty simple, and clearly not an easy mark to ever approach, more or less fully inhabit this vision, and we can.

While this vision is the top of the top, what are the critical building blocks that create a solid foundation to both enable and empower any one to inhabit self-responsibility or self-accountability? Consider seven keys to get in gear and count on yourself as your own authority in life:

1. Presence, that is, the experience of living in the present moment:
Only by showing up in this here-and-now moment can self-responsibility and self-accountability come on-line and be authentic. Also add the complementary skill of witnessing, that is, in presence standing aside to observe who we think we are (the imaginary or false sense of self or ego) to reveal, see through and dissolve its false authority and fear-driven influence.

2. Honesty, that is, telling the straight-up, nothing left out,

truth in life:

Purely by playing with a full-deck in being a stand-up guy or gal can anyone take responsibility and accountability for his or her own life.

3. Stalwart, that is, exhibiting solid, stable and disciplined words and actions:

When anyone has genuinely traversed an extended learning curve, much like learning in the trenches of long, hard and smart work and often as an apprentice with one or more mentors, whatever abilities truly built and owned communicates a solid, stable, disciplined and aware sense of oneself in having some clear idea what makes you tick.

4. Congruent, that is, words, actions, facial expression, body language and tone of voice all communicate the same message of clarity:

When one's whole body and being sends a singular and un-divided message across all levels of expression, what gets trans-mitted is something greater than the sum of these parts-it com-municates a trust and confidence that what is seen, heard and experienced is real, authentic and true.

5. Not knowing and being open:

To bring the maturity to fully value not knowing and staying wide open translates into being available to all inputs, creativity, possibilities, brainstorming, innovation and perspectives on life working, all of which are core attributes to bring in developing self-responsibility and self-accountability.

6. Win-Win/Non-Zero-Sum Game:

Being a mature grown-up entails shedding the me-me-me primitive ego's attachment to itself and playing a much bigger game of what works for everyone, literally a win-win or non-zero-sum game. Here one brings an attitude of no scarcity of anything and a surplus of everything for everyone to meet life's demands.

7. A rock-solid commitment in action to grow:
Possibly the rarest character trait on the planet for human beings to bring-a rock-solid commitment in action to grow. To bring the publically stated intention to grow, a time and place for this to occur, and the follow through in direct actions to completion.

The three components of a commitment and when accomplished on a regular basis pointing to a committed person, self-responsibility and self-accountability are palpably self-evident.

There is no stopping such a being in any set of circumstances in powerfully harnessing and channeling their energies, talents, skills and abilities in transforming and transcending all obstacles in ever-arriving and inhabiting their full creative expression.

This may well be the greatest personality attribute and character trait you can bring to any transformational process, whether expressed in a therapeutic process, meeting the highly challenged circumstances relationships regularly present, or in effectively facing and dealing with change in its multitude of disguises however it arises in this present moment.

Have you ever considered what would allow you to die peacefully and even joyously? This may seem like a morbid question to ask, yet only by making peace with death can anyone fully live. Since it's only the ego-mind and body that dies, and not who any one of us truly is, this takes all the pressure off.

Some of the most admirable, impressive accomplishments blossom from the most everyday activities. Begin by inhabiting presence, witnessing the ego-mind and living your Authentic Self.

Next, see the possibility of being a really wonderful offspring to your parents and an equally tremendous parent to your children. Add the possibility of being a loving, understanding, patient and supportive partner in your committed intimate relationship.

Include the further opportunity of being a terrific, loyal and truth-telling friend to another human being. Consider having made an authentic contribution in having truly touched others and having left some enduring legacy of achievements or your presence itself.

What a wonderful addition to this handful of marvels to honestly be a whole human being, having built strong internal strengths and a capacity to bear strong emotional states, in truly being an adult. I'm game. Are you?

CHAPTER TEN

HOW BE THE GUY IN THE ROOM THAT CAN HANDLE ANY EMOTIONALLY CHARGED UPSET OR CONFLICT WITH ANYONE PART 1

Love, acceptance, respect, to be desired, security, passion, are all things a woman may want in her relationship. As a matter of fact these are basics that probably everyone wants. There are certainly others and each person has specific desires. What I want to focus on here is the specific aspect of emotional safety in relationships.

The challenge in satisfying this desire is that the feeling of "safe" is sometimes generated from opposing dynamics, and this can create conflict. How a woman feels with a man can change moment to moment depending on these opposing forces This can lead to confusion about what she wants. It can also confuse the man as she appears to want two different things. If we become aware of the conflicting beliefs paradigms this can begin to make a lot more sense and clear up the confusion.

First let's understand some of the aspects that create a feeling of safety in a relationship. A man's unconditional acceptance of a woman means that there is no judgment and criticism.

She can communicate honestly, be herself, and feel emotionally safe. There are also physical and financial factors that can appeal to a woman's sense of safety.

Sometimes a woman will trade one of these comforts for another in her relationship. It is emotional safety that I want to address. It is the one that creates a great deal of confusion.

A confident man creates the feeling of trust with a woman.

A woman will feel emotionally safe with a man who is emotionally available, honest, trustworthy and authentic. These are emotional character strengths she can respect and admire in a man. A man of character and emotional depth is a man who knows who he is and likes himself.

His love for himself is so strong he does not need to gain the acceptance of others by trying to be something he is not. His strength is not physical so much as it is in the clarity of his mind and emotions.

These are character strengths that a woman not only admires, but feels safe with. He is not a weak man that will bend to the whims of other people. She can trust him to be who he is. I describe this kind of man as being in his emotional integrity.

A woman feels safe if she believes the relationship is going somewhere.

A different factor for women that creates safety is her trust that the relationship is solid and will work out. When a man spends time doing activities as simple as cleaning house and cooking together it sends a message that he is committed to being with her.

It is wasteful to invest her time with someone that may be gone soon. You want to know if your prospective partner has the capacity and willingness to match you for a deeper emotional commitment.

There is also the fear that if after getting emotionally invested in a man there will be a break up. It makes sense for us to wonder where the relationship is going. Sometimes a woman wants to be "safe" from the potential pain of a broken heart.

She wants to avoid the emotions associated with being alone.

This kind of safety is really about protecting herself from the painful emotions that come from her fears of break up and being alone.

When a man is distant emotionally or physically from her it may bring up feelings of loneliness, or fear of a break up. Seeking this type of emotional safety can lead to emotional drama.

Fears and insecurity in relationship takes a woman out of her emotional integrity.

In order to avoid her fears of being alone the woman may make efforts to keep her man close. It might be a criticism for going out with the boys for an evening. By discouraging him to do other things she is increasing their time together.

A critical comment is a means to reject his behavior so he would avoid criticism in the future. Becoming sad is a way for the man to notice her and get what she wants. If there is a lot of emotional charge the dynamic might include anger or jealousy.

It is possible the man ends up feeling guilty for having done the "wrong" thing that caused her to be upset. The man may want to avoid the night out with the boys just so he doesn't have to deal with her emotional reaction.

The Downside of getting what she wants

If a woman engages in such efforts and is successful in controlling her man she will have influenced his behavior by her emotional reactions. With influence over his emotions she will have influence over what he does with his time.

He will learn to avoid the activities that bring emotional reactions and criticism and do the things that she approves of. They will spend more time together which will help her to feel solid in the relationship. It also distracts herself from the fear of being alone.

In one part of her mind she has helped their relationship, but she has unknowingly created a separate feeling of not being safe.

When a woman see's that she can modify her man's behavior she might perceive him as not being as strong. She will see him as someone that gives up his interests, runs around trying to make her happy.

He has stopped being his authentic self and started being what she wants him to be. At some level she perceives him as no longer being his own man. She could perceive him as having weak character and could lose respect for him.

More importantly she will not feel safe with a man she sees as having a weak character. Some women will conclude that if they can influence or control their man then other women will also be able to control and influence him as well. All of this adds up to losing respect and trust in the man.

One assumption sometimes deep in the mind is that the stronger person controls the weaker person. If she can direct him then he must be weaker than her.

This image of weakness is amplified if the woman already considers her self as weak to begin with. The loss of trust in her man's strength may not be conscious to her, but at some level it affects her feeling of safety with him.

On the one hand the woman has driven her man to be near her so that she can feel secure in the relationship. On the other hand because she now perceives her man to be controlled by her emotional reactions she no longer sees him as a solid foundation of strength.

Desire for closeness is from our emotional integrity but can also be from fear

A woman's desire to be in close companionship with a partner can come from her emotional integrity. The desire to spend time with a partner to have fun and create together can be completely authentic.

When in her emotional integrity the sense of safety she feels is normal because together they are a stronger force than if she were alone. She is out of her emotional integrity when her motivation for time together is for protection from fears of being alone.

A woman in her emotional integrity is free to ask for what she wants, and that includes spending time with her partner.

It can sometimes be very difficult to discern whether we are acting on behalf of what we desire, or on behalf of fear avoiding. One way to measure is to observe the emotional reaction when we don't' get what we want.

The situation looks impossible. If the man acquiesces he may appear weak to her. If he doesn't then it appears that he doesn't care.

For the woman it is also impossible. If she doesn't make an effort to bring him close she may feel fearful and uncomfortable with being alone. If she works to keep the man close she is acting out of fear and runs the risk of being controlling and losing respect for herself and her man.

Giving up limiting fear based beliefs

It only looks impossible if we limit our options to the compensating strategies of control. If we are to find true happiness in our relationships it will require dissolving the beliefs and assumptions that create the painful fears and controlling behaviors.

We will have to seek an emotional solution beyond what the mind offers as safety from fear.

Great Love in Relationship is present when there is no fear

The fears of being alone are coupled with assumptions and beliefs about the experience and ourselves. Those beliefs usually involve not being good enough, unworthy, self rejection, and other people rejecting us.

This is the painful emotion that people are seeking protection and safety from. These beliefs are lies and only exist in the mind. Just for starters there have been many times when we have been alone and been happy.

We have just learned to associate being alone with misery. When core beliefs of self rejection are dissolved there is no longer any fear of being alone and there is ample room for self acceptance and self love.

Changing beliefs also eliminates the need and behavior of being controlling to our partner. Great Love thrives in the absence of fear.

What motivates the man to be with his woman?
There is ample material here to talk about the man's half of the relationship. The man's motives and his integrity with himself are completely unknown. He might respond to the request of his woman just because he loves her and desires her to be happy. In this way he is completely in his emotional integrity.

However a man that is uncomfortable with her reactions or feels guilty may be out of his emotional integrity. Even though his actions to be with her are the same the motivations are different.

What is happening in the man's mind, beliefs, and emotions is a completely separate dynamic. This example has more to do with the woman's perception of her man, than the man himself.

In my perception a small percentage of men actually live in their emotional integrity. It is the man's loss.

Not only is the emotional quality of life much more beautiful, but it imbues to a woman something that is very attractive to her.

In the depth of her emotional integrity a woman desires to be with a man of emotional depth. Not all women are comfortable here but at some level they are yearning for a deep emotional connection.

A woman can choose to wait for a man with the character and integrity that she respects and wants. But as she waits she should prepare herself as well. Being with a man of integrity will not be like being with other men.

He will be seeking a partner that will treat him with the same level of unconditional love with which he treats himself. If she brings her judgments, fears, and emotional reactions to the relationship, he may decide that he would rather be with someone else.

When a woman asks where the relationship is going there are often different parts of her asking. Authentically she will want to know if the man has the emotional depth for greater commitment, or if fear keeps him trapped.

But she might also be asking because her fears are driving her mind to search for symbols of safety in relationship. In this case her motivation to know may be more about fear than about depth.

As you begin to evaluate these elements in your relationships, begin by asking what your own motivations are. To do this effectively you will need to be aware of your emotions and not the story in your mind.

The story in the mind is too often the denial system or one of the transient voices in our head. You will be much more effective in being aware of another once you become self aware of your own emotional motivations, and beliefs. Whenever you evaluate your relationships, begin by looking at your half.

To gain mastery over your half of the relationship, including your perceptions, expectations, thoughts, beliefs and emotions, begin by practicing the exercises in the Self Mastery Program.

My perspective comes from working with women clients over the years to identify and change some of the core beliefs that sabotage their relationships.

Any description of a group is never completely accurate as each individual is different. I share this here for people that find it valuable in understanding their emotional dynamics or that of their partner.

CHAPTER ELEVEN

When you were growing up, how did your parents or other caregivers handle conflict?

1- Did they fight when they had conflicts?

2- Did they ignore the conflict, hoping it would somehow get resolved?

3- Did one give himself or herself up to avoid the conflict?

4- Did one get angry and the other shut down?

5- Did one get angry and the other comply?

6- Did they discuss and resolve their conflicts, caring for themselves and each other?

Unless you saw them do the latter, you had no role modeling for healthy conflict resolution.

All relationships have conflict. Conflicts are a part of life and can provide an opportunity for learning and growth — if they are approached with caring for yourself and the other person. How two people in a committed relationship handle conflict is often an excellent indicator of the health or dysfunction in the relationship.

Conflict can trigger many fears — fear of rejection, fear of engulfment, fear of being wrong, fear of losing a battle, fear of getting hurt. When fear is activated, many people go into the "fight, flight or freeze" stress response.

When the stress response is activated, the blood leaves the brain, organs and immune system and goes into the arms and legs for fight or flight. The blood leaving the brain makes it hard to rationally think things through. Therefore, trying to resolve a conflict when the stress response has been activated doesn't work well.

What Not to Do

If one or both of you are triggered into fear, here is what not to do:

1- Don't escalate the conflict by attacking and blaming.
2- Don't fuel the flames by defending or explaining.
3- Don't shut down and withdraw.
4- Don't try to pacify the other person.
5- Don't comply. Don't give yourself up.

If you do any of these controlling behaviors, you will either escalate the conflict into a fight, or you will lose yourself. In either case, there will be no caring resolution.

What to Do

There are only two responses in conflict that have a chance at leading to healthy resolution:

Opening to learning
Lovingly disengaging
Learning

If neither you nor the other person is triggered into your fears/stress response, then you can open to learning. What this means is that you become curious about your own and the other person's reasons for each feeling the way you do.

When you each share your point of view, with caring for yourself and the other person, you each open to the possibility of learning something new.

By each of you opening to seeing the situation through the

other person's eyes, you will each likely gain new information that will enable you to resolve the conflict in a way that works for both of you — where neither of you feels you have given yourself up or compromised yourself.

Even if one of you is triggered into the stress response, if, in your experience, the person is often able to get themselves back into some calmness and caring, you might be able to say something like,

"I really would like to understand your point of view, and I hope you want to understand mine so that we can resolve this conflict. Would you be willing to explore this with me?"

If you say this in a calm, loving tone, this might help the other person to calm down and become open to learning with you.

Disengaging: Disengaging is completely different than withdrawing. When you withdraw, you are shutting down, closing your heart, cutting off your love for yourself and the other person.

Withdrawal is a form of punishment: "I will shut down and withdraw my love from you until you stop hurting me, or do what I want you to do."

Disengaging is temporarily leaving the conflict, but keeping your heart open to yourself and the other person.

This means that you need to learn to lovingly manage your painful feelings of helplessness over the other person being closed, and of the loneliness and heartache that might be there when someone is angry, blaming or shut down to you.

A powerful way of managing these painful feelings is to put your hand on your heart to ground yourself in your body, and fully acknowledge the feelings with compassion for yourself.

Compassion is a very powerful energy, and when you acknowledge your feelings with compassion and understanding, you will find that they start to dissipate.

When you disengage, you might say to the other person, with a kind and open voice, "I don't think we will get anywhere right now. Let's try again in half an hour and then maybe we will be able to be more open with each other."

If you were triggered into fear, then once you have compassionately acknowledged your feelings and allowed them to move through you, take some time to understand what might have triggered your fear. Understanding this will help you begin to heal the triggers so that eventually you can stay open in conflict.

Once you feel fully open, go back to the other person and see if he or she is ready to learn with you. If not, then you will need to let it go for another time, or even let it go permanently. We cannot have control over whether or not another person opens in conflict.

If the other person doesn't open, then you will need to decide for yourself how to take loving care of yourself in the face of not being able to openly talk about the conflict.

If you practice these two healthy behaviors each time you get stuck not being able to resolve a conflict, you will find yourself feeling better and better — even if the conflict doesn't get resolved.

Most conflicts are fairly easy to resolve when both people are open to learning about themselves and each other, and are caring about their own and the other's highest good. Attempting to resolve conflict when one or both people are not open is generally a waste of time.

You might find a way to end the conflict, but it likely will not feel satisfying to one or both of you — especially if one wins and the other loses. This is especially difficult in a primary relationship, and will eventually erode the connection and intimacy.

Often, when one person changes the system by moving into the intent to learn and/or lovingly disengaging, the whole system improves.

It's worth a try!

CHAPTER TWELVE

QUALITY TO POSSESS

Maybe some of you have come across the term of being an Alpha Male. In fact, there is plenty of material that suggests to simply copy what an Alpha Male does and all your problems with women will be solved. But what if some of the true characteristics of an Alpha Male don't necessarily involve being as unpredictable, outspoken, or as egotistical?

1) He Is a True Leader

True Alpha Males are more commanding in their presence than they are with their mouth. Alpha Males are not necessarily the loudest guy in the room, the one with the most to prove, but he is the one that when he speaks - has an audience that is willing to listen.

He is the one that "people" go to, because its "his" opinion which is the one that counts. In other words, he leads and commands the respect of the room.

And that is truly what a leader is. A truly great leader isn't someone who just tells you what to do. A true leader is one whom you trust, listen to and respect. One in which part of you admires. So how does he display this dominance.

He could do this in a number of ways which he can demonstrate this which includes, directing the conversation, asking questions, doing things on his terms (at his convenience), moving with intent and purpose, communicating in ways that are magnetic and powerful (through body language and tone of voice) and very aware of personal space and ignoring its boundaries (touching them when communicating others, positioning themselves closer to someone) and so on.

2) He Listens and Responds

A true Alpha Male has the ability to listen and respond in equal proportions to his ability to lead and dominate. He earns the respect, admiration, and attention of the people around him because he can presently and actively engage them in any moment.

And these people, can and will feel his "presence" while conversing or being around him. That's what makes him magnetic. And that's what makes him attractive to women.

3) He Engages in Minimal Approval Seeking Behavior

He has a strong sense of self, that is not dependent on the opinion of others. This can sometimes be seen and described as confidence, but it is so much more than this. Confidence can sometimes be faked. True self assurance cannot.

This also enables him to truly do that which he desires. He takes in information from other people, their opinions, and their actions but ultimately will come to his own conclusions.

And most of the time, these conclusions can be directly in contrast to the opinion that he was presented. This isn't about always being right. This is about being rebellious or disagreeable.

It's about the fact that he draws his own conclusions and stands by them. This communicates a sense of autonomy and independence. Which in turn communicates strength in character.

4) He Has Above Average Self Esteem

Part of having high self esteem involves: being confident to speak your mind, express your opinion, give an apology when one is needed, learn a lesson where one is due, or call another person out on their own limitations.

He is going to tell you the truth. When he feels like telling you the truth, which most of the time will be in that moment and he will not make any apologies for it. And it will be insightful and it will be brutally honest.

This is what women appreciate. Because she goes around in her day to day experience with her friends, co-workers, and family - dishing out sh*t tests, brattiness, and occasional flakiness because she gets away with it most of the time.

In fact, for some women it's a tried and proven method. It's worked for her time and time again. So here comes this guy, who calls her out on her actions instantly.

Maybe it was something that she said, maybe it was something that she did, but the end result is the same. She is either gobsmacked, or she is incredibly impressed - if not both. And she won't know exactly what to do.

One, because she didn't realize how much she had been misbehaving and two because she so rarely gets called out on it. So now here is guy who seems, calm, relaxed and who can see her for who she really is, or at least a part of her that no other man or person has been so quickly able to identify.

And that is why a true Alpha Male is so attractive to the opposite sex. Because the sense of who he is and how he behaves, triggers multiple attraction points in a woman that put her at "his" very whim. But that's where she wants to be anyway.

In this way you can learn to become a true man who helps the women you are pursuing be able to fully experience themselves as true women. So, what are you waiting for? Give it a go!

The Ultimate Players Or Lovers Nice Guys Are

There is a lot of talk about The Ultimate Players lately:

Who is The Ultimate Player?
What Can I do to become The Ultimate Player?

I have personally never hidden my disgust and disdain for so-called players or pick-up artists. I find them to be modern world's scum of the worst kind, mainly because many of them deliberately try to destabilize, degrade, or diminish another person's self concept, world view, emotional control, awareness and interpretation of reality, in order to gain advantage over that person.

And please don't give me that crap about "women who want men they can dominate". I come from generations of warriors - 7 foot tall, all lean muscle with (you-know what) danggling all the way to the knee.

Brave warriors who fight lions with just a spear (they don't come any more masculine than that!). The lowest low any warrior can go is attack someone who has fallen down. It is considered cowardice of the lowest order - one not even a scavenging vulture or hyena can stoop down to.

Let me back up a little. There are two kinds of "Nice Guys." There is the "Nice guy" who is thoughtful, confident (emotionally, physically and sexually) and can be relied on to take charge and get things done. He is called "Nice" because he is sensitive, attentive and considerate.

In other words he doesn't pretend to be the Alpha Male because he is also in touch with his feminine side. This is the rare breed of men. And ladies, if you've got one, hold on tight.

Then there is the "Nice guy" who exhibits some even slightly non masculine (and nonsexual) tendencies, which typically arise from a desire to be "sensitive, attentive and considerate" but quite often backfires because "Mr. Nice" often confuses "spineless" with "sensitive" and attentiveness with indecisiveness.

These are guys who may have been raised by females who were very manipulative and controlling and as a result these men have not learned healthy ways of relating to women.

But that's not the worst part, these "Nice Guys" have also become great at playing the "victim" role and use this to manipulate and control women in the worst possible imaginable ways.

Maybe you will say, "Wait a minute. Nice Guys could never ever manipulate or control a woman. They are the victims here".

And that is where you are dead wrong. It might surprise you to learn that just as 'Players" advertise themselves as "Alpha Males", these "Nice Guys" advertise an identity of "Weak Victim."

"Alpha Males" pride themselves in persuading and breaking down resistance by use of "domination". "Nice Guys" use "victimization" which interestingly appeals to women who have that natural instinct to "mother" and often want to "rescue" and "take care" of this poor, misunderstood, mistreated and abused "Nice Guy". This is the "Nice Guy's" position of power and control.

But I have to be fair. These "Nice Guys" on most part are not themselves even aware that they are caught up in the unconscious desire to feel victimized. All they know is that they're always clinging to the women that they're afraid of losing.

They are always clinging to any slight indication of friendliness on a woman's part. They will stalk her, beg her, turn themselves inside out and even kiss ass, if that is what it takes for her to look their direction.

They seem to never get a break, at least not enough "love" for them to feel like "not victim".

Like any kind of manipulation it comes back to bite "Nice Guy" ass, same as the "Alpha Male". Manipulative techniques attract equally manipulative women.

If you are acclaimed "Nice Guy" and really tired of chasing, begging and clinging, realize that it's never too late to change.

Stop looking at your struggles right from childhood as "only pain and suffering" and realize that, that same pain and suffering also have endowed you with a sensitive side and has brought you in touch with your feminine side which is a very attractive quality to women - especially when it's not overdone like you do.

Give up the pride of feeling victimized, along with your secret hope to taste revenge for all the hurt and abuse you have ever suffered - and you could be living the relationship of your dreams. Meanwhile Mr. Alpha Male continues his quest for world domination! Ha

CHAPTER THIRTEEN

SUPPRESSION OF THE ALPHA MALE

Prior to the 1970s, role models for young men were plentiful. Their attributes were well described and positive. There were examples of successful men shown in many situations: head of family, business and political leader, sports participants, doctors, lawyers, assembly line workers, minors, airline pilots, explorers, military people, etc.

There were self-improvement and further education plans as well as manual skill development programs and technical education schools, all mainly developed around what the male would need In order to support a family.

The role of males and females in American society was pretty much settled. The leading/ building/ creating/ directing types of vocations were mostly peopled by men.

Women were mostly shown in support roles for men and rarely in positions of leadership and/or decision maker.

This portrayal of women's role in society was by and large due to the majority of them being house wives and mothers, and even though the role played by women while being the house wife and mother also involved, in many cases, handling the family finances, that was not considered a skill set.

Women worked in, among others: nursing, medical technologist, secretarial, wait staff, organizing, teaching in primary and secondary schools.

Were those types of vocations peopled by women because of their free choice, or was it because of societal pressures?

The reasons for those choices of labor can be debated although there is objective demonstration that early on in life most females lag behind males in innate spatial and logical cognizance.

The need to be in control of her situation and being competitive was not recognized outside of the family situation.

Their physical strength being only forty percent of men led to them being viewed as less capable for vocations which required physical strength. Did all this lead to women looking for work in other than technical disciplines?

Women were viewed as the supplicant gender in sex. Men were seen as the aggressor which led some to miss the point that in other than rape cases females are the gender which controls when and if sex occurs.

She was also expected to comply with his expectation for sex which also led to the misconception of the male being dominant.

The reasons for the choices back then are important for this article only to draw context for looking at how things have changed since those days and accessing what the impact may be of these changes on males.

Minority groups within society began getting more attention while gaining a greater part to play in societal decision making as women rose in prominence.

There have been several minority groups identified: Women, people by place of origin [Latinos, Asians, and the like], Blacks, Disabled, LGBT people and some others.

Recently there have been very bad actions by younger males which resulted in deaths of innocent people and I'm left to wonder if the societal changes over the last five decades have played a part in those actions.

I believe the primal urges within males are still strong and a driver for their actions. They still strive to be leaders among men and demonstrate this through making nearly every activity competitive. They still feel they play the role of protector of 'their' female, if modified.

That 'their' female should look up to and respect them. They think they should be the decision makers in their relationship while conceding the woman's things, such as decorating the abode and controlling the house hold issues, to 'their' female and that they are to be the ultimate disciplinarian in the family.

Their image, as they see it, is still that they are head of the relationship with 'their' female. They fall back on sports to bolster this. They still believe they voluntarily concede leadership to 'their' female and that society as a whole supports that belief.

Weakness in a male is a very bad attribute. It diminishes his very reason for achievement and his feeling of self-worth suffers.

Males have always dealt with rejection by females of their advances but they still had the strong leader role models in the media to look up to and be impressed by. This is no longer the case.

Television is the main source of input to society. The participation of women, LGBT people and minorities in the world of advertising has replaced that of heterosexual males.

The decision making process in marketing and advertising is strongly influenced by women and LGBT groups and begs the question: has the result grown to where heterosexual alpha males are the subject of derision or suppression? It seems as though that may be the case.

The portrayal of the sexes on TV impresses society with what the genders should be. An example is the female complaint of the desirable female: slim, physically fit, well proportioned, and beautiful.

As for the young male: gone are the strong role models; the clear thinking, decision making heroes he imagines his role to be. He does not have an area of activity which is free of females.

There is no place where males can be males without the effect of female disapproval of his priorities and value system. In nearly every advertisement, and most of the sitcoms on TV the male is portrayed as a bumbling idiot, incapable of existing without a female to make decisions, protect and defend him.

Even in the world of sports the reporting and discussion programming is no longer men's province. Although the sport is contested by men, women, some who do not even play the game, now lead the discussion panels and news reporting, replacing the men who once did that.

The young man needs role models, not anti- alpha male models and not simply men who excel at a game.

With only impressions of inadequate males and the leadership of females on TV, and in some cases, his mother leading the family, the young male has nowhere to turn to legitimatize his need to be a competitor.

Does this diminish his achievements; his sense of self-worth? Is achievement academically an alternative? How does he deal with the frustration? What role in society does he see for himself? How would he act out in this situation? What effect might that have on the already difficult need for gaining respect from males and attracting a female?

For soldiers in the battlefield there is a lot of hurry up and wait. So many times they are forced to sit on their ass only to see a little bit of action now and again. Thus, one gets complacent and the fear, which ramps up alertness, also turns to mush.

Unfortunately when a lackadaisical attitude sets in it can be dangerous for the soldier and his lack of alertness can in fact get himself and his comrades killed, not good.

There is a way to stop these issues from killing our troops. No, we probably cannot stop the boredom, but we can bring things back into perspective a whole lot faster and even skip the response time which comes from the sounding of bull horns or alert systems. How so you ask?

Well I propose a brain wave electronic pulse sent throughout the base camp, military base or outpost. This alert would be an extremely low frequency but would peak the brain to the ultimate alert status and simultaneously accelerate a primordial innate brain response of the Alpha Male. A fight response brain wave alert system is what I am referring to and

I believe we currently have the technology to make something like this a reality and it would save lives in the battlespace and could become a very important part of our future force allowing our organic response to coincide with first alert sensors in the net-centric fast pace game of future warfare.

CHAPTER FOURTEEN

Everyone wants to develop a lean muscular physique. The quickest way to get there and stay there is via resistance training. My favorite style of resistance training is old school weight training accompanied by the sound of clanging plates with heavy loads on a barbell.

Do you know who trained/trains like that? Arnold, Zane, Reeves, Coleman, and Cutler are a few of the guys with that training mentality. What do you think of their physical development? These men have mastered the Alpha Male Physique.

Though a well balanced physique is essential, nothing screams Alpha Male Physique like a HUGE MUSCULAR CHEST. Let's look at Arnold... arguably the greatest chest of all time. How did he get there? He trained with intensity.

He trained with power. He trained with a goal in mind. He trained with real deal heavy weight Home Gym. The result was a chest that made history. As far as I'm concerned, if it's good enough for Arnold it's good enough for all of us!

There are many maximum lift milestones along the way of building your ultimate alpha chest. Oftentimes 135 lbs, 225 lbs, 315 lbs, 405 lbs and even heavier weights are popular goals that we aspire to conquer at one point or another during our training careers.

Others take more of a "pound for pound" approach to measure their success. Some people have the goal of benching their bodyweight, 1.5 times their body weight, or even twice their body weight.

Most of the time when people talk about this, they are talking about their Flat Barbell Bench Press One Rep Max. This is a great exercise and a good way to establish quantitative goals; but, don't forget the ultimate goal.

The ultimate goal is a great chest... not just moving a certain load on the bar (unless you are a power lifter). The great chest you are going to create is a result of more than just the development that comes just from Flat Bench.

So how do you develop your most impressive chest?

You need to pack on lean mass and slash excess fat. Like the greats, you must move serious weight and focus on training all areas of the chest. Often people do just flat bench and forget about the variations to get well rounded results.

To put on slabs of pectoral beef you must hit flat, incline and decline chest movements. Time and time again you will see chests that look like ski slopes. There are two reasons for this. The first reason is simply excess adipose tissue.

Extra fat on the chest it tends to collect at the lower portion of the pec area. This creates the "slope effect." To lose this one has to lose total body fat.

The second contributor to the "slope effect" chest is that the mid and lower portion of the pecs are somewhat developed; however, the upper portion is severely underdeveloped. This is a result of doing just flat bench and neglecting incline movements.

You combat this and build your alpha chest by following a well designed chest training program that puts an appropriate emphasis on the upper chest, mid chest, and lower chest.

One way to ensure this is to start one out of two or two out of three chest workouts with the emphasis on the upper portion of the chest. To place more emphasis on any particular muscle group simply start the workout with exercises that are specific to that area.

Because you are fresh at the beginning of the workout the results for that area will often be greatest. I suppose by now you are looking for a killer Alpha Male Chest Workout? Well here you go!

Sample Workout

Month One
Incline Barbell Bench Press: 3x 15-20 reps
Decline Barbell Bench Press: 3×15-20 reps
Flat Barbell Bench Press: 3×15-20 reps
Feet on Bench Push-Ups: 2 sets of MAX reps (one minute rest between sets)

Month Two
Flat Barbell Bench Press: 4×10-15 reps
Incline Barbell Bench Press: 4×10-15 reps
Decline Barbell Bench Press: 4×10-15 reps
Hands on Bench Push-Ups: 3 sets of MAX reps (one minute rest between sets)

Month Three
Incline Barbell Bench Press: 5×5-10 reps
Flat Barbell Bench Press: 5×5-10 reps
Decline Barbell Bench Press: 5×5-10 reps
Regular Pushups: 4 sets of MAX reps (one minute rest between sets)

Now you know what to do. How do you go about getting it done? You need the proper equipment. There are many options out there; but, don't be fooled by inferior products. Make sure to invest in a bench that can handle the weight you can do today and more importantly the weight you will be able to do tomorrow.

Also chose a piece of equipment that offers versatility while maintaining the integrity of each position. Often companies cut corners and the functionality is sacrificed for increased versatility.

When it comes to a piece of equipment that is both functional in all positions and versatile, which leads me to the most fit equipment for these kind of workouts.

More versatility exists because of the dual sided racking station posts. You can use them for holding the barbell elevated to shoulder height for squats. Or you can rack a loaded barbell at hip height for rows, or deadlifts from the opposite side of the bench. No matter how you look at it there are numerous options and no excuses when using this sturdy and versatile bench.

No more excuses! It's time to make it happen and create your Alpha Chest.

Premature Ejaculation Exercises

Premature ejaculation exercises are the only, and easy way to gain natural male enhancement. The process doesn't just stimulate the senses, it promotes growth in all the areas that men seek after, and it does so without pills, pumps, or other non-working methodology.

For those that are looking for the ultimate solution, it has finally arrives and many men are going from zero to hero in the bedroom in just a few minutes time.

One of the most heavily advertised products in the world is a solution for erectile dysfunction. However, despite the solution working for a few hours, it leaves many men wanting more.

Masking the problem isn't solving it, and for men that deal with premature ejaculation and sexual dysfunction, it can be even more stressful to find out that the solution they've chosen has harmful side effects.

Some of the major side effects paired with chemical solutions include, high blood pressure, stroke, heart attack, color blindness, and complete blindness. Those are hard prices to pay for sexual stimulation, but some men seem to think it's the only way.

It's important to understand that it's not the only way, as there is a better path to male enhancement.

Premature ejaculation exercises are non intrusive, easily done in minutes, is effective for an extended period of time. By isolating the root causes of sexual dysfunction, you can easily become a stud in the bedroom.

However, before you can utilize exercise to promote quality love making, you need to understand what the root causes of disorder are. The first cause is over sensitivity of the area.

Many men climax too soon because the penis is sensitive, forcing the body to naturally want to promote finishing. The second root cause is lack of bodily knowledge. Penile exercise promotes a solution for both, naturally, and effectively.

The penis is made of chambers that fill up with blood when aroused. Exercise and stretching the tissue promotes cell generation and growth. It also reduces sensitivity to the area, and helps a man control the mind, giving a sense of confidence that lasts through the years.

It's important to understand the exercise plan does not promote arousal, but rather promotes steady stimulation of the cells and chambers that make up the interior of the penis. This is not a chance to start masturbating, and it shouldn't be seen as such.

Premature ejaculation can be thwarted; it just takes some commitment and discipline. Like a professional athlete trains daily to become the best, a man should train to be better in bed.

Training doesn't mean long hours of working out; it's just a matter of a few minutes a day, working on a concentrated plan of action to please their lover easily.

It's important to understand that sexual performance is not just physical it is mental as well. If you can rule over your thoughts, and combine that with natural male enhancement, you can really see a wealth of good. However, if you try to stimulate one without the other, you will be back at square one. It's important to gain mind control, and physical control for long lasting results.

CHAPTER FIFTEEN

CONCLUSION: BECOMING THE ALPHA MALE - THE SECRET TO DEVELOPING A CONFIDENT ALPHA MALE MINDSET

Women love alpha males. It's not like it's a secret or anything. They are irresistibly attracted to the leader of the pack, at least the emotionally stable women, the women you want.

An alpha male epitomizes masculinity. He is a leader in life and confident around women and people in general. Women want to be around him because he makes them feel good. Ultimately, these are traits you need to develop and hone over time to pull that sexy kitten and keep her purring for as long as you want.

The key element that separates an alpha male from the so called "beta male" is his mindset. Your chance of success with women and dating is directly correlated to your attitude.

Consider the following two examples:
A frustrated geek: "I feel nervous. She is going to know I'm nervous. What if she rejects me? What if people see me being rejected?"

Rampant thoughts like these are often running through the beta male's mind. This kind of negative attitude causes him to lose the game even before any attempt has been made.

The lack of confidence seeps out into his body language and mannerisms. Women can sense this a mile away and his chances of success are lowered, significantly, even before making a move.

Conversely, consider the following example:
An alpha male: "I'm a catch. I have nothing to lose and everything to gain by approaching that foxy blonde. If she rejects me, that's her loss."

In this example, the alpha man has a strong positive attitude. His mind is clear, free of self-limiting beliefs. Even if he does get rejected, he has already created a type of inner shield against rejection.

Before delving into the nuts and bolts of meeting women, you should first spend some time to focus on yourself, not on women.

What happens on the inside is usually a better determiner of success than what you say or how you look like on the outside. Learning and developing an alpha male mindset is the first step to improving your dating reality and getting the results you deserve.

Thoughts Are Real

First of all, understand that thoughts are real. Thoughts tend to manifest themselves in the real external world. For example, think sports psychology in which athletes use positive visualization to physically and literally improve performance. Anything that you think of or imagine can be realized externally.

Your thoughts also directed related to your emotions...
Emotions are extremely powerful drugs running through our system. They tend to manifest themselves in our communication (verbal and non-verbal), voice tone and overall personality, however subtle.

We all know how hard it is at times to hide feelings of nervousness or insecurities. There is a very real and strong connection between your habits of thought and who and are as a person. You really are what you think you are.

Secondly, you need to take responsibility for your own thoughts. Understand that you, and ONLY you, are responsible for your own daily inner dialogues.

Once understood correctly, this is a very empowering realization. Why? Because it means that you do have a certain level of control over your emotions, and can therefore choose the type of person you want to be.

So, how exactly do you develop this alpha male inner game and become an alpha male, the person women instinctively respond to?

Remove Self Limiting Beliefs

Before you can reprogram your mind into a more confident alpha male, you will need to develop awareness of your daily thought habits. Pay attention to your inner dialogues that are constantly running through your head day to day.

Writing your daily thoughts down in a journal is helpful in keeping track of your inner game progress. You'll discover that you do have control of your thoughts and how they can change over a short period of time.

Before you can remove any self limiting beliefs, you first need to develop self awareness.

1- "Life sucks".
2- "I hate my job".
3- "Girls don't like me".
4- "She will probably reject me anyway".
5- "She probably already has a boyfriend".

Repeating negative self talk such as these examples above tend to pile up in your subconscious mind. Repeated negative thoughts become harder to undo as time goes by. The longer the negative habit, the harder it is to overcome it. Think of it as a river. The longer this river stream flows, the deeper the tracks are imprinted and the longer it'll take to get the water flowing out in a new direction.

A simple, yet effective technique you can use to remove these self-limiting beliefs is by consciously replacing them with positive affirmations. Take the example "I am becoming an ultra confident alpha male."

At first, your mind might reject this thought because it's not used to you saying it. However, try repeating this phrase for a couple minutes, several times a day, for a couple weeks.

Then one day, you will catch yourself doing something that you have never done before, like walking up to that hottie sitting in the coffee shop and naturally initiating a conversation.

It's very important that you visualize and feel your affirmations for maximum results. Just repeating an affirmation, without visualizing and feeling it will not help you much.

Whatever thought you'd like to become reality, repeat it in the affirmative as opposed to the negative. For example, don't say "I am not afraid to approach women." Your unconscious will ignore "not" and the words "afraid" will constantly be drilled into your mind and associated with "approaching women."

Instead, try using something like "I enjoy approaching women." Over time, the mind will start to anchor "approaching women" with the word "enjoy" instead of "afraid." Then, once you've finished approaching that girl in the book store and had sometime to analyze your performance, you are more likely to remember the experience as "enjoyable," regardless of how well it went.

The new experience will mold in a new, more positive mental "river stream" and you will be more likely to approach another girl the next time. Your new, more constructive mental thought becomes habit and the previous negative mental habit fades away.

You become more emotionally intelligent and your confidence is raised. The positive cycle then deepens with added attempts, further increasing your self esteem and attractiveness to women.

The best time to train your mind with affirmations is before falling asleep. This is best since your body is most relaxed and your mind is most receptive, easily accepting thoughts as reality.

Give it a try, but you might need to give it some time before you notice results, especially if you've your glass is half empty more than not.

OTHER BOOKS
BY BRYAN

MY GIFT TO YOU CLICK THE LINK BELOW

https://nowthis.life/rac/

PLEASE WRITE A REVIEW!

If this book helped you out in any way, please help me to help others by writing a review!

https://www.amazon.com/dp/B073S7Y435

Still, if you did not get anything new from this book or you were not impacted in some way, I would still like to hear what you have to say. Either way, I will know what am doing right or wrong and to improve in the future. I wouldn't like to take your money and not deliver. So please, take just 2 minutes to let me know what you think.

Everyone is searching for help on how to improve their lives for the better and one thing they do look for are reviews. If this book has a lot amazing reviews with great comments, they will buy the book and read it and so the ripples effects of goodness spreads. But if it doesn't have any great reviews and comments, they don't buy the book and read it.

I know this book can positively impact and help someone and you can help that person by writing your thoughts and takeaways from the book.

Additionally, I would like to read your review and hear how this book has helped you in any way at shape or form. My plan is to print every single review and hang them on my home office wall to read for inspiration and motivation throughout the day.

Your great review helps me personally to stay focused and be able to validate all the hard work and lots of hours invested in preparing this book for you.

https://www.amazon.com/dp/B073S7Y435

Thank you again for reading this book and all of your support, I am truly honored and grateful to have been of help. I look forward to helping you make this year the best ever for you and your family!

OTHER BOOKS BY BRYAN

The Female Logic

When You Suck at Dating

www.ingramcontent.com/pod-product-compliance
Lightning Source LLC
Chambersburg PA
CBHW061359250726
48657CB00004B/1569